# THE MASCULINE

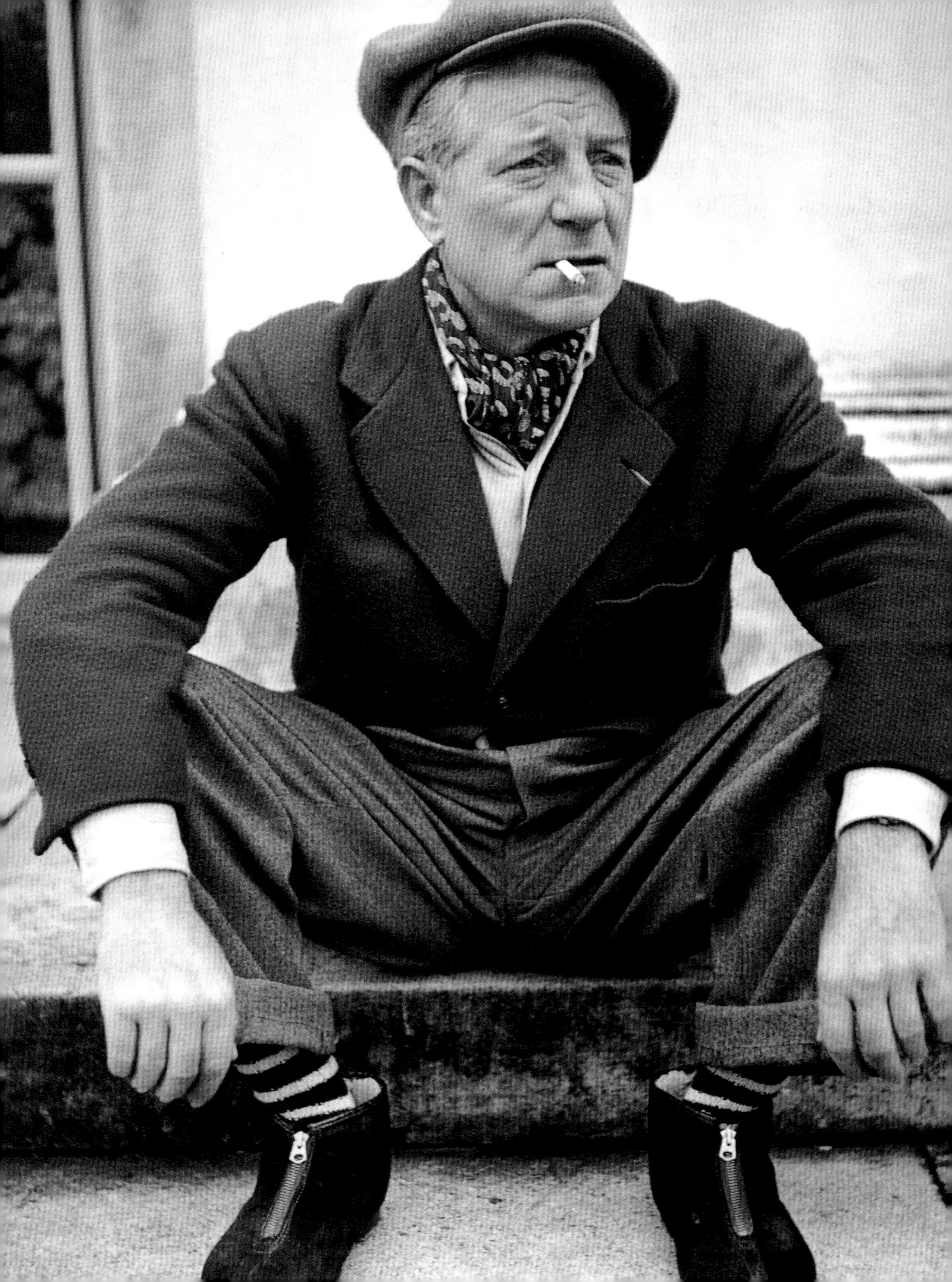

# THE MASCULINE

RICHARD KEHL

DARLING & COMPANY    MMIV

INTRODUCTION

This is a companion volume to *The Feminine* (2002). Here, as in that book, I attempt to shed light on this mysterious universal through a gathering of images in which the pairing and sequencing are crucial to my meaning.

The following, from my introduction to *The Feminine*, is equally true of *The Masculine*: "Neither the images in this book nor the few words – these included – try to explain or analyze the feminine. Rather, they embody it." The difference in the approach of the two books is, hopefully, the difference between these two polar embodiments. *The Feminine* draws upon what I take to be feminine qualities: "receptivity, quietude, a close connection to the rhythm of being, a sense of wholeness, a preference for the intuitive." *The Masculine* proceeds from such masculine inclinations as planned action, focused will, logic, and concrete manifestation.

The masculine spirit, as the feminine, is present in both men and women. I hope that these two books will deepen one's awareness of these twin elements, and will lead to a richer appreciation of their places in human wholeness.

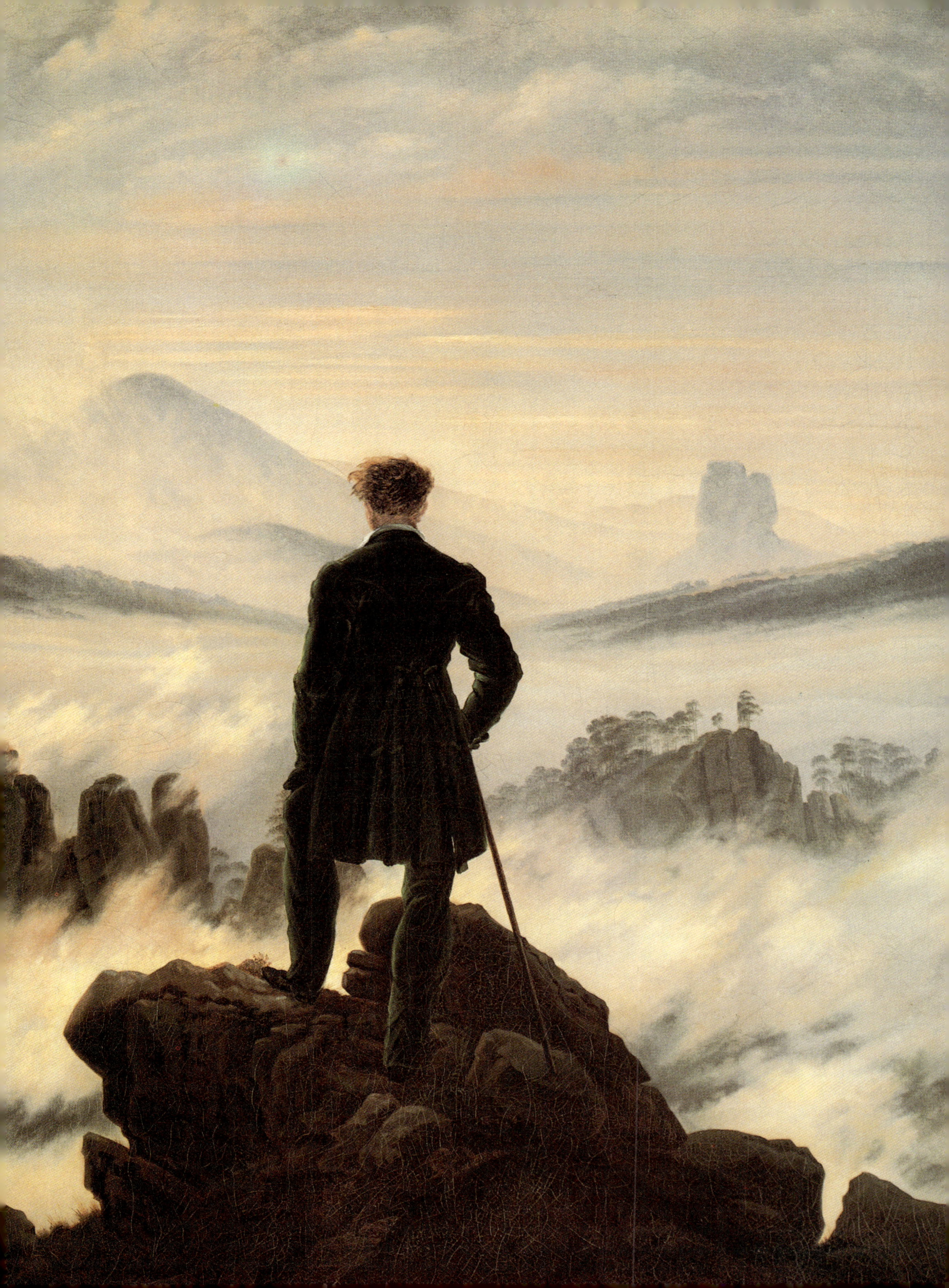

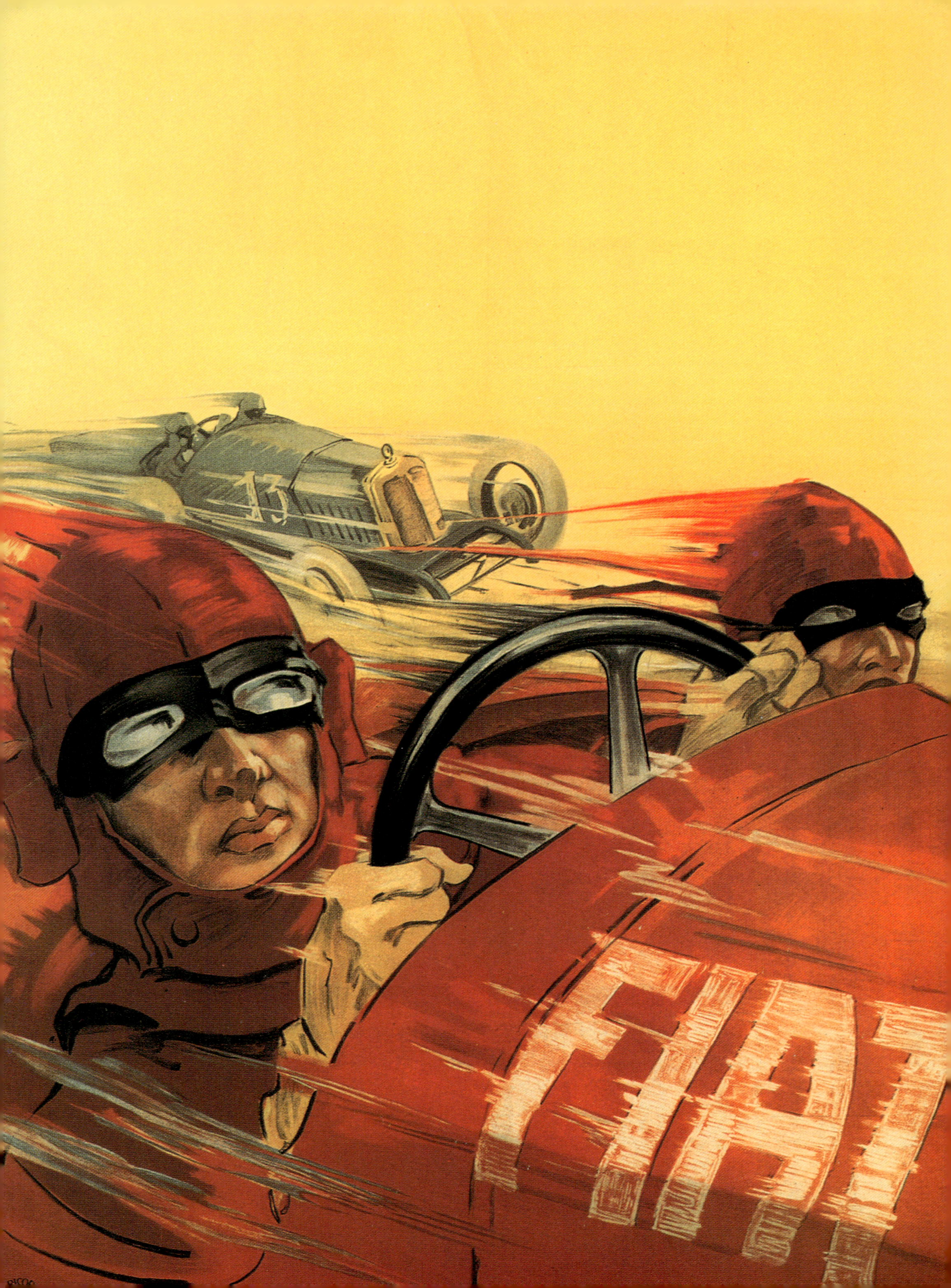
13
FIAT

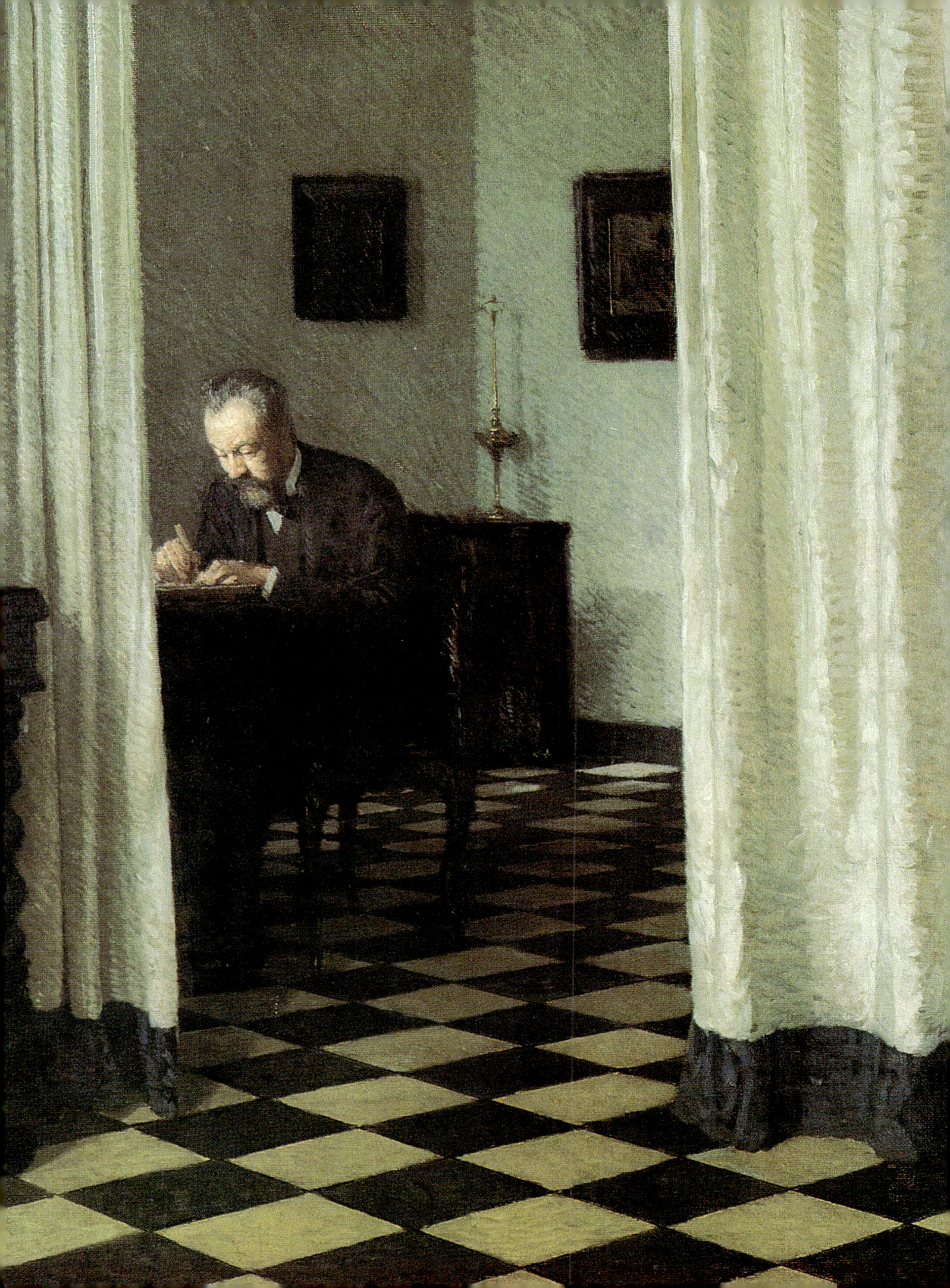

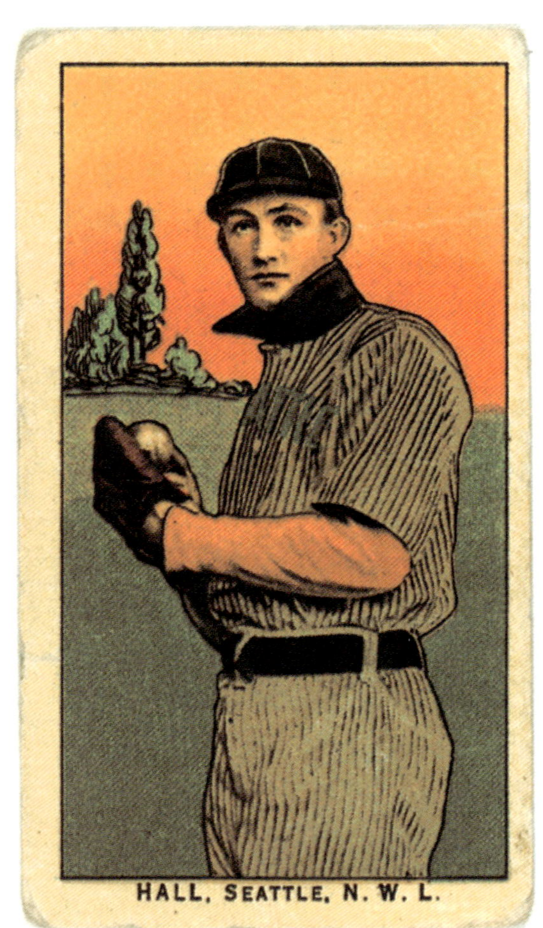

HALL, Seattle, N. W. L.

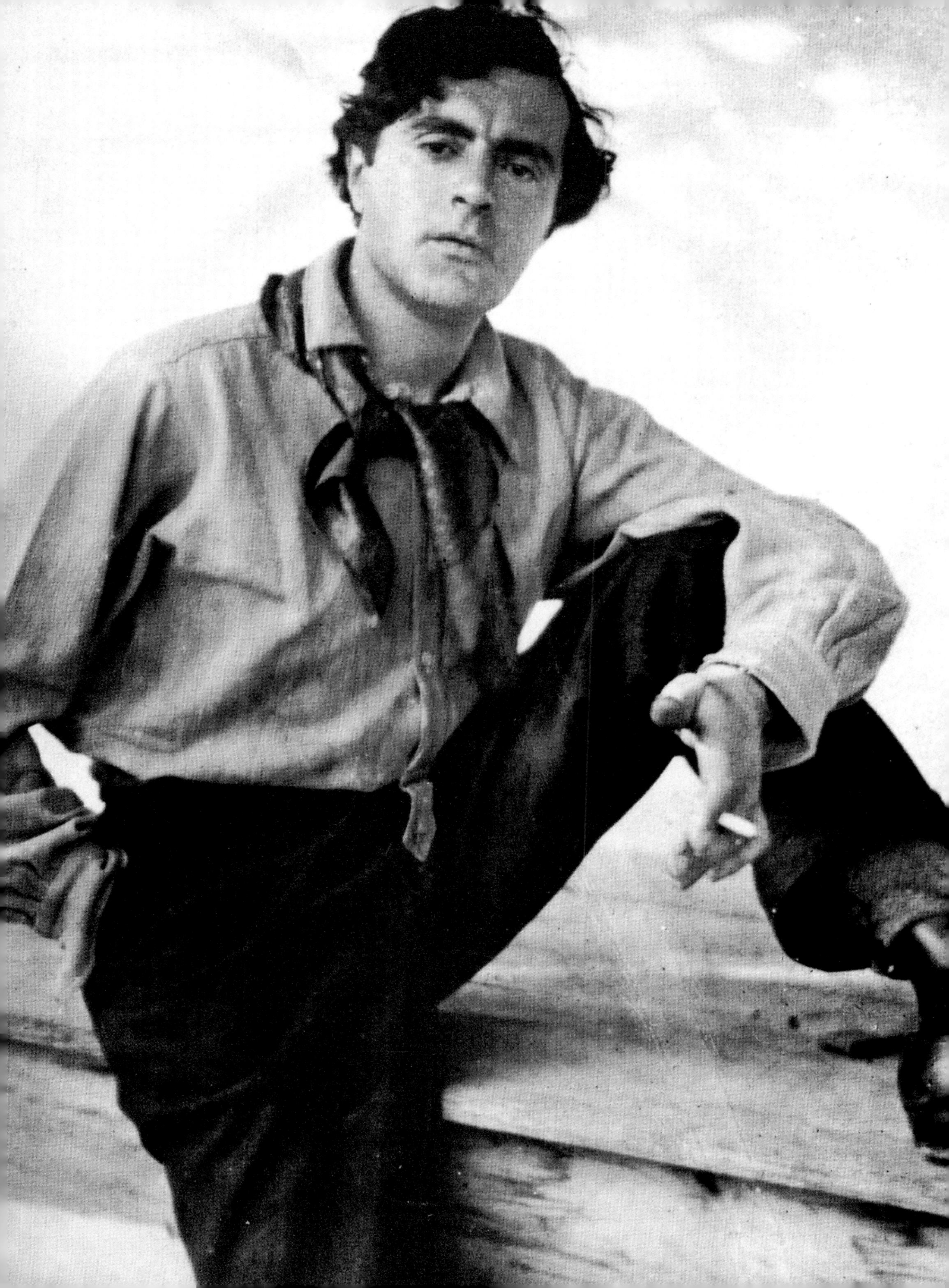

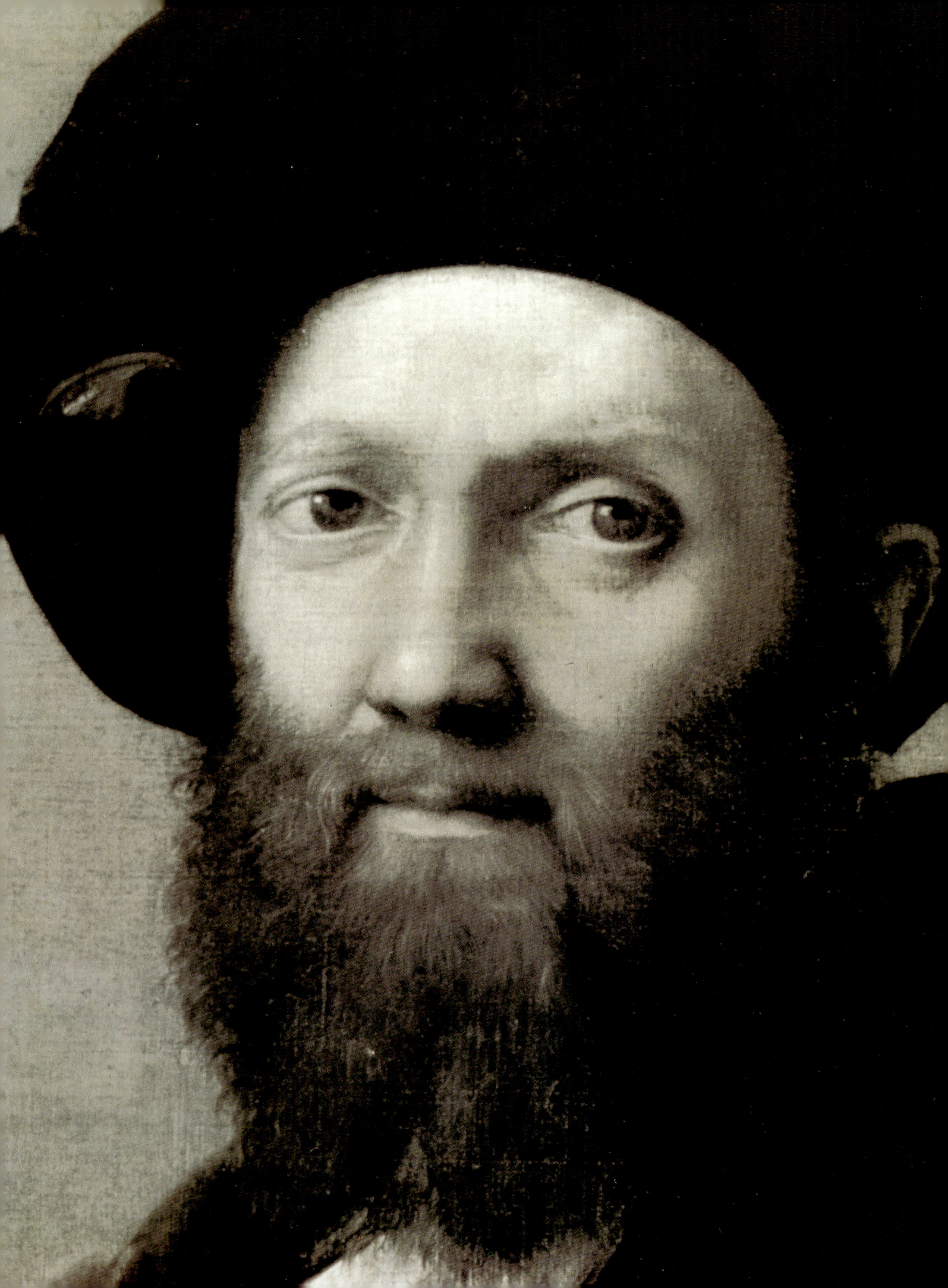

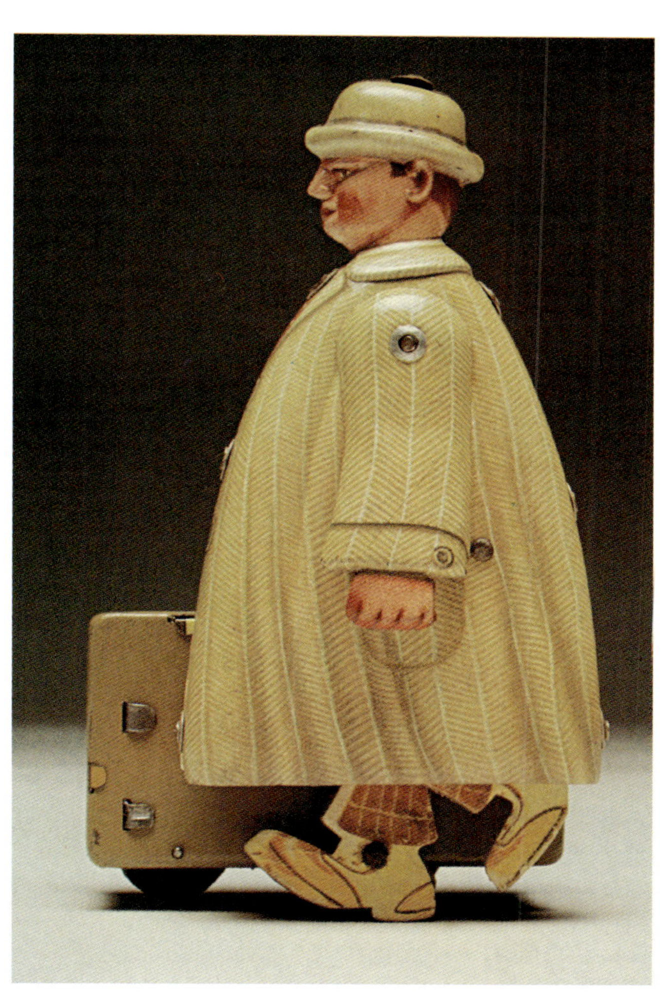

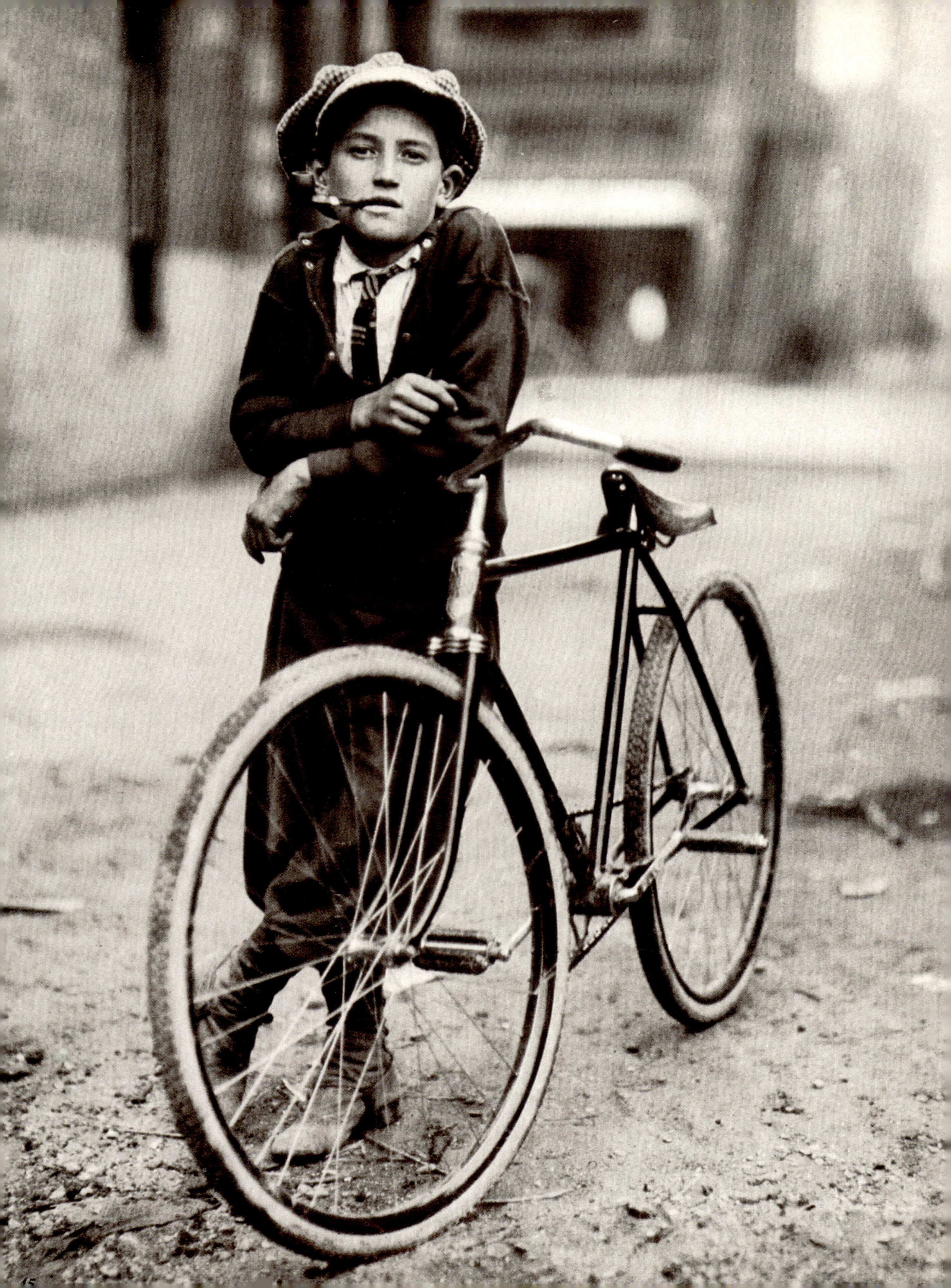

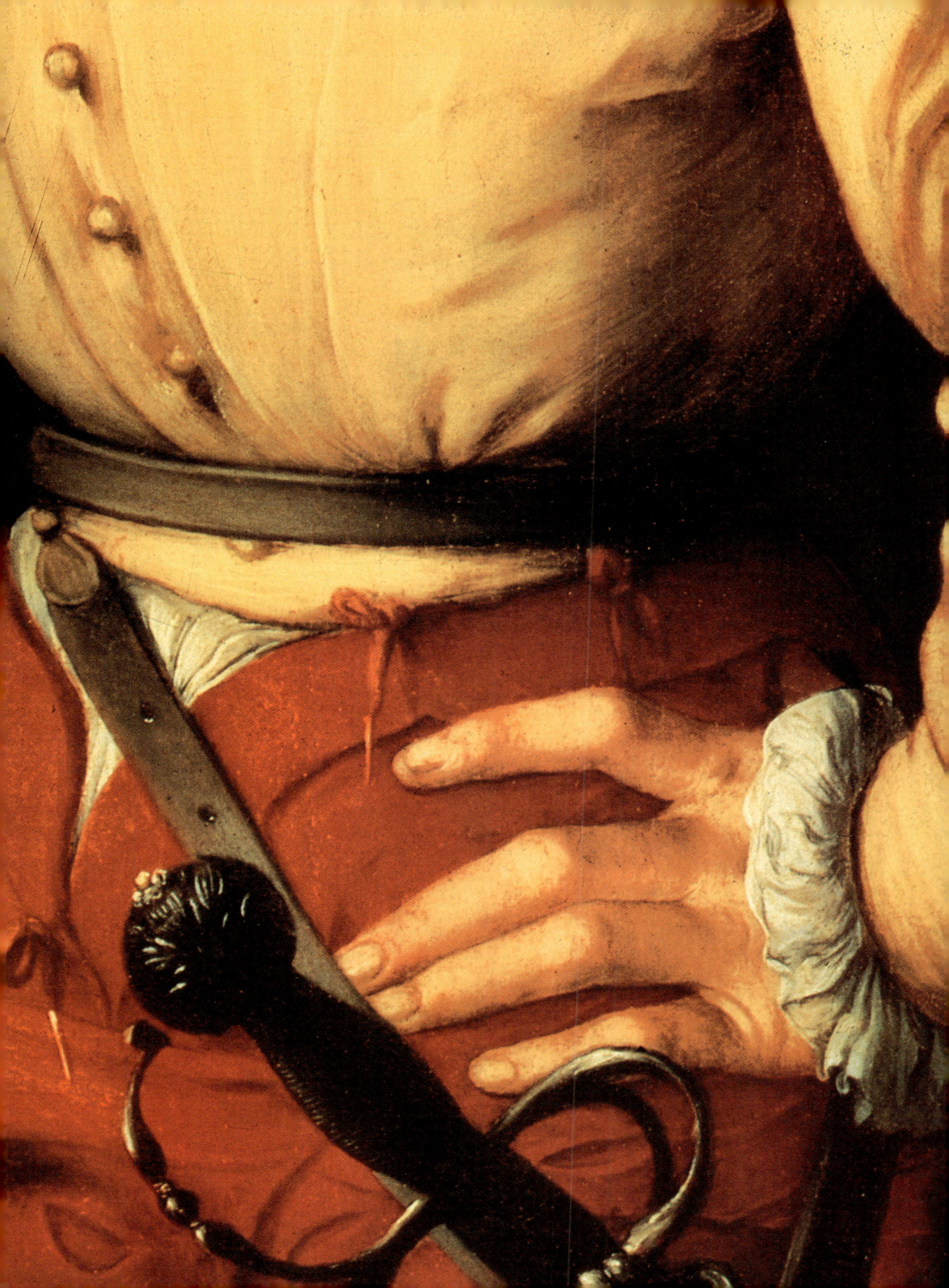

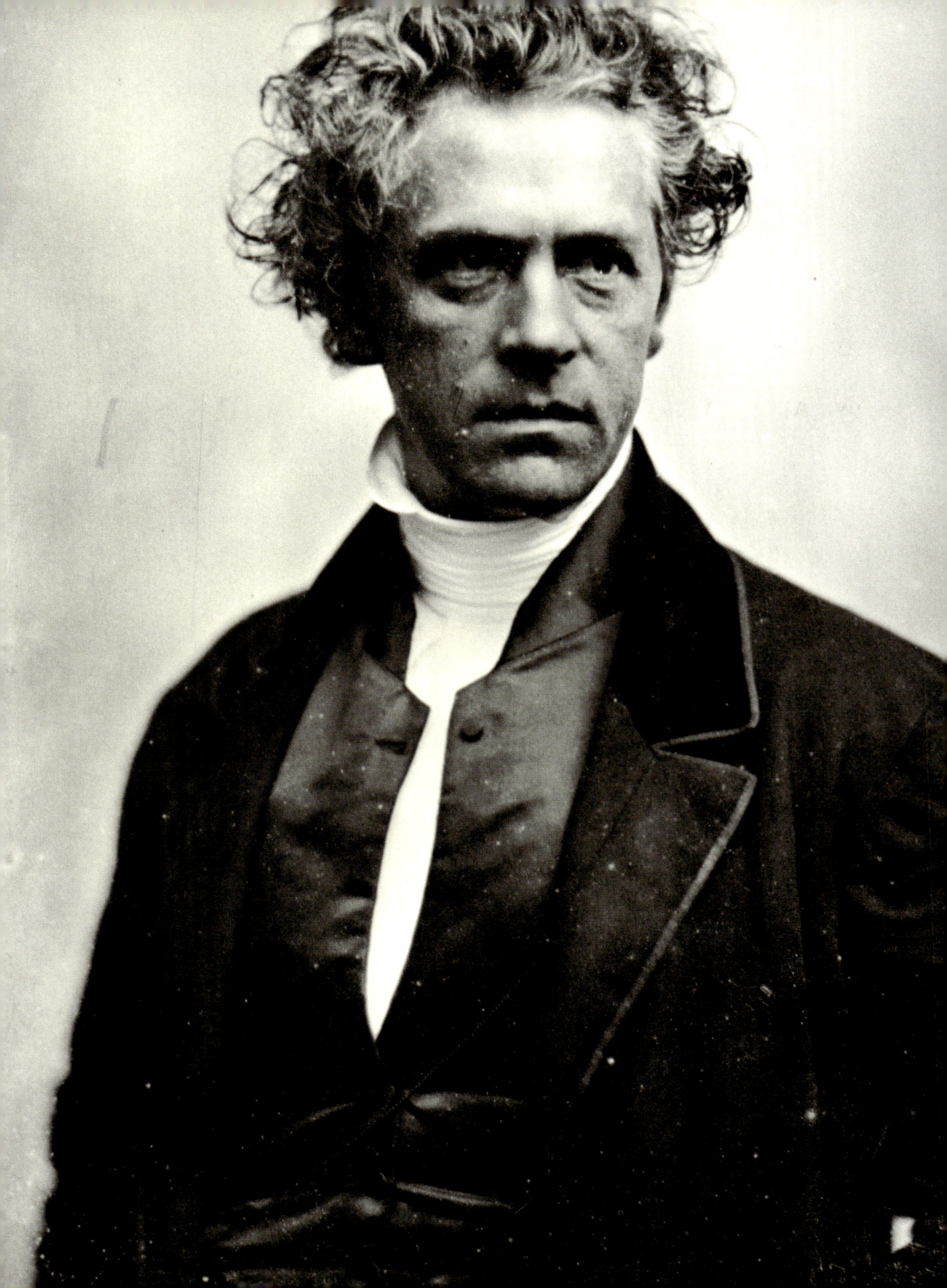

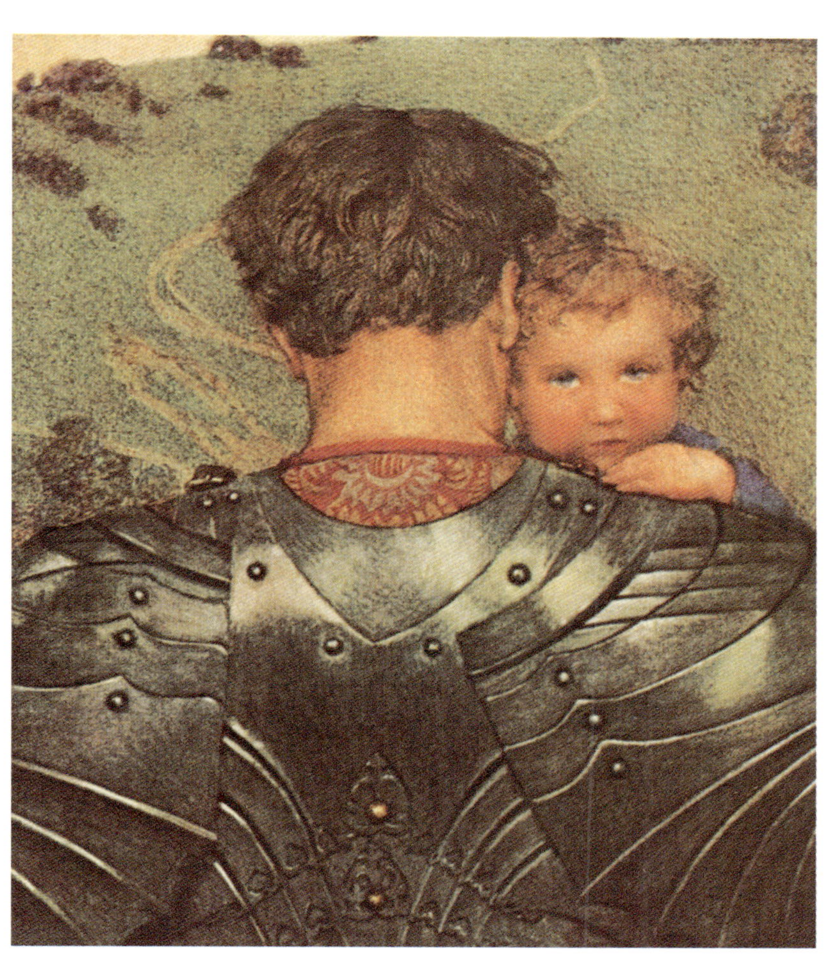

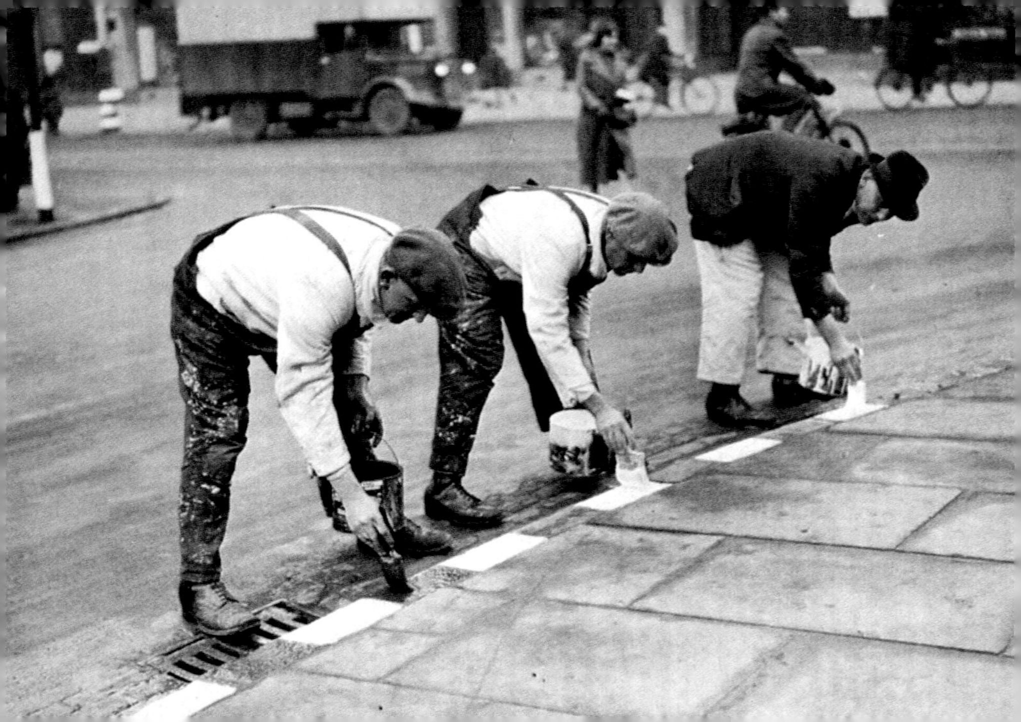

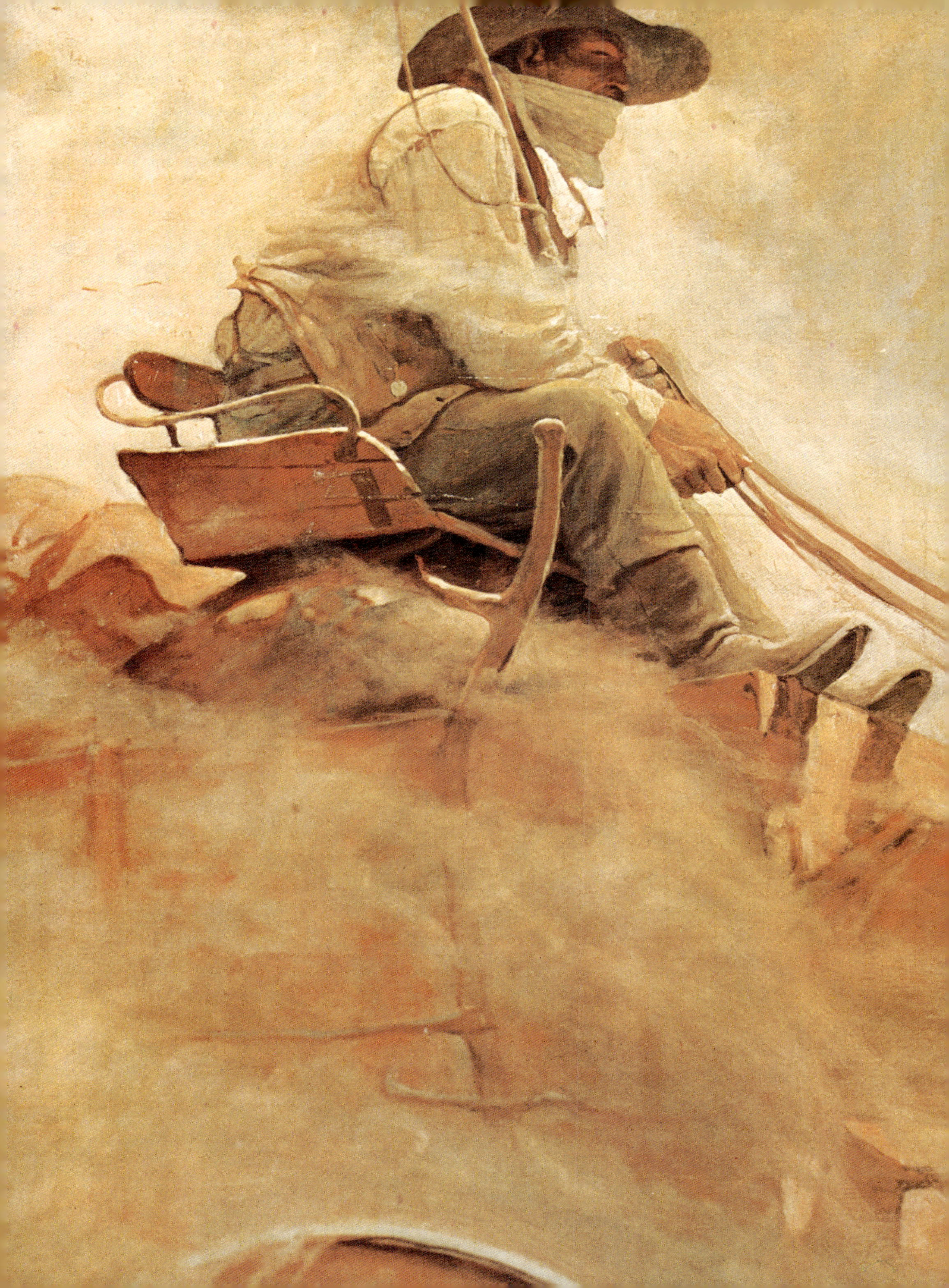

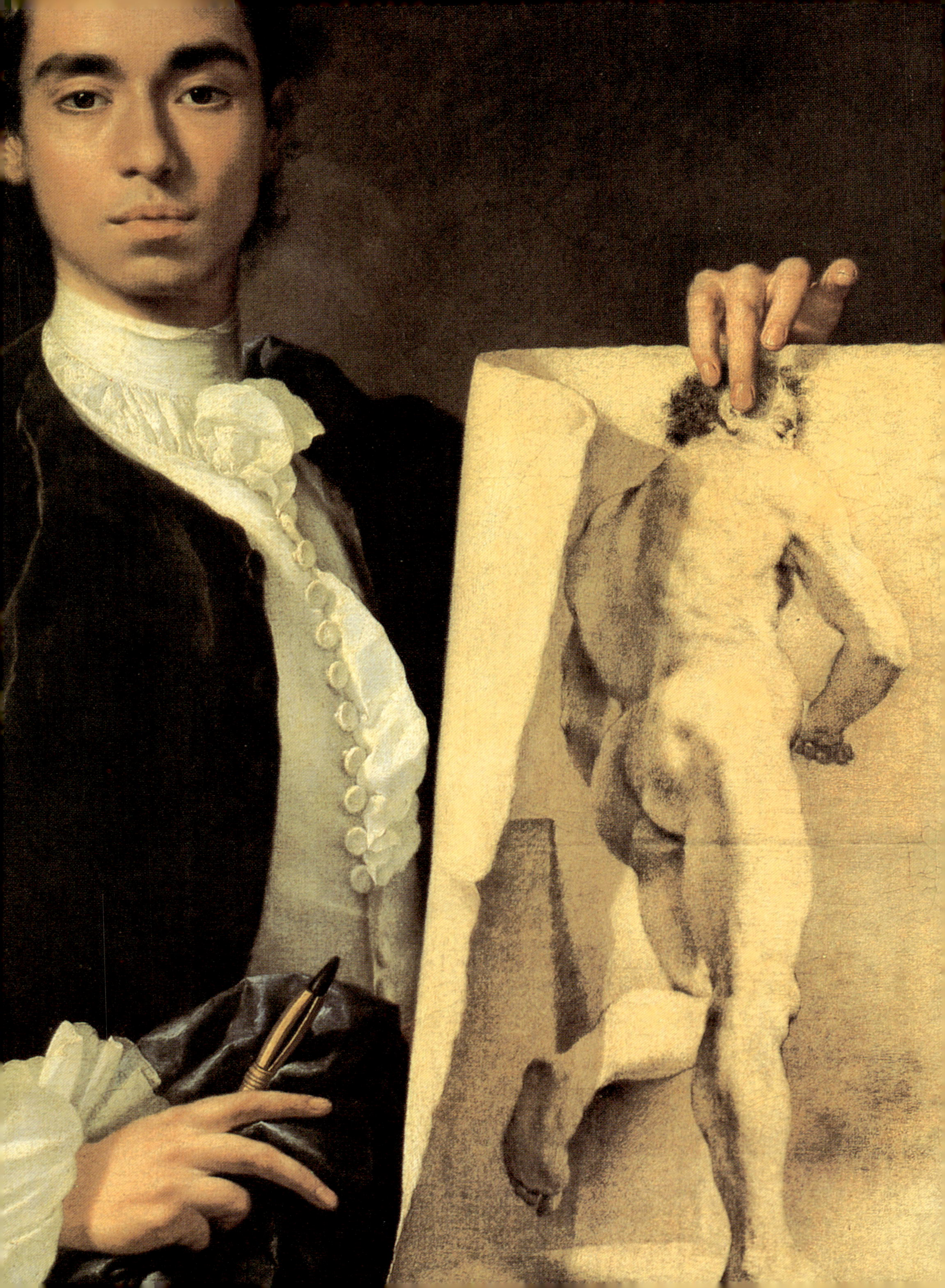

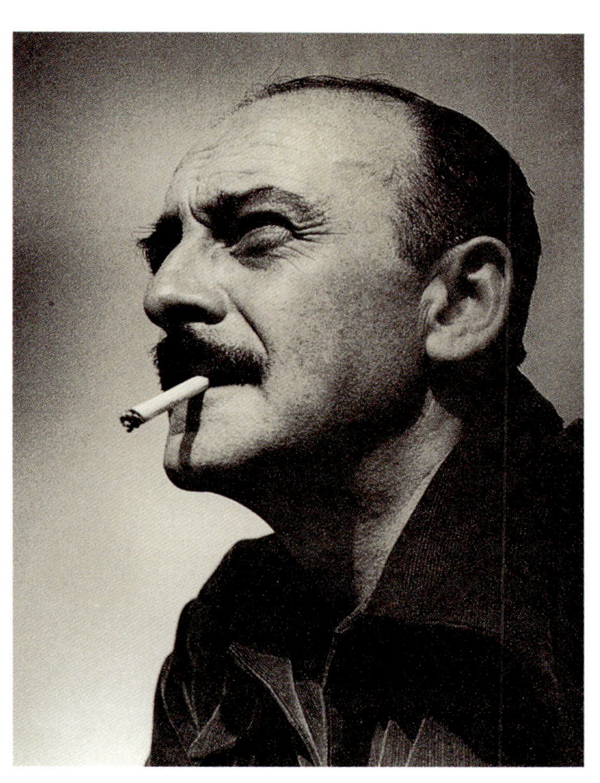

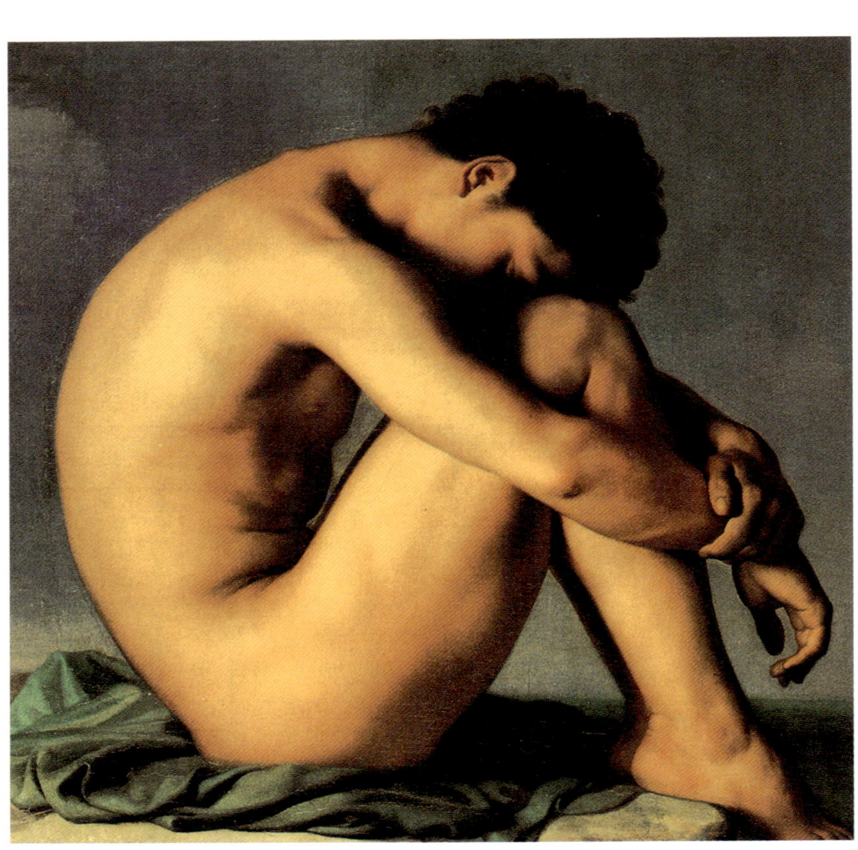

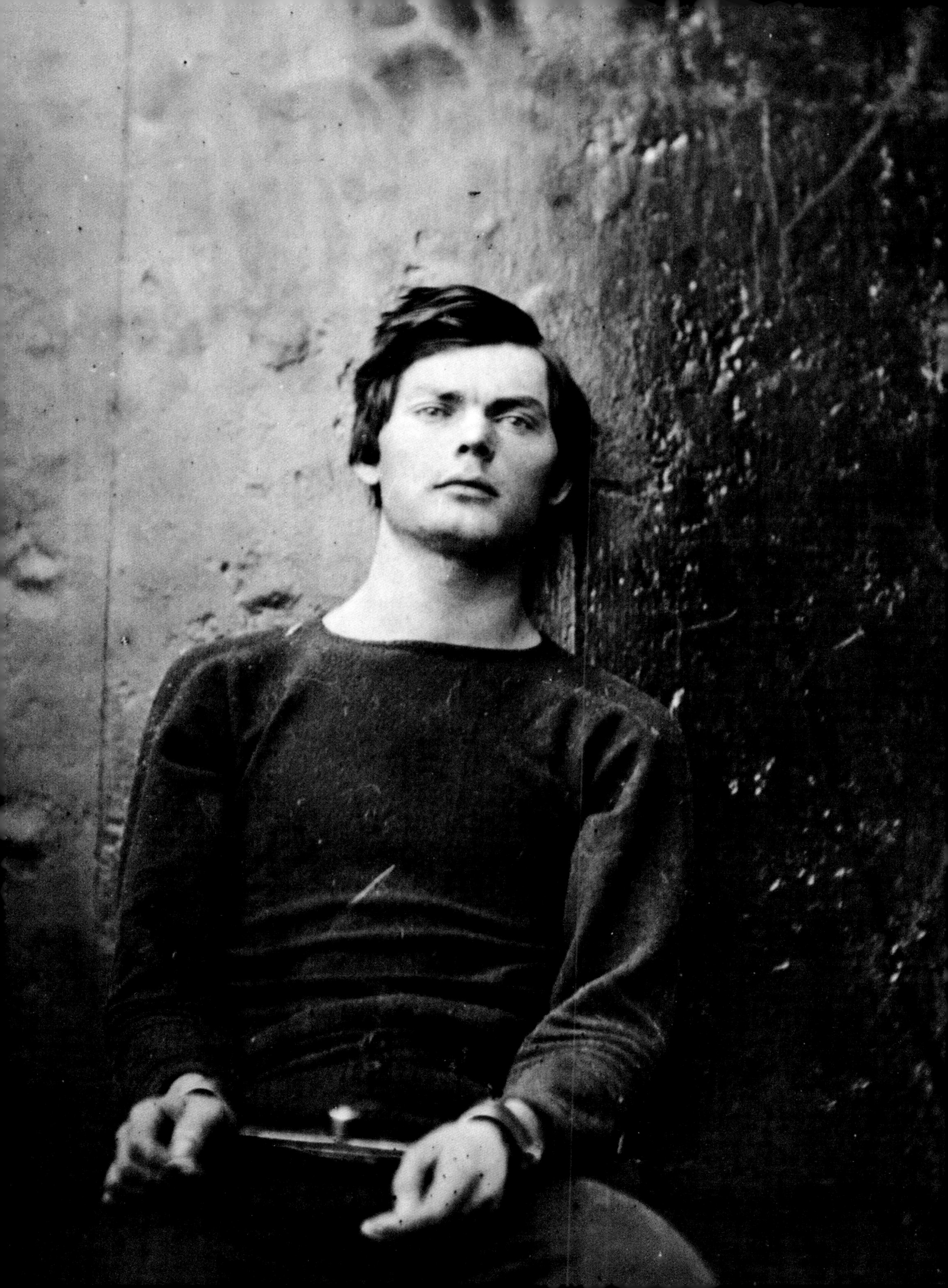

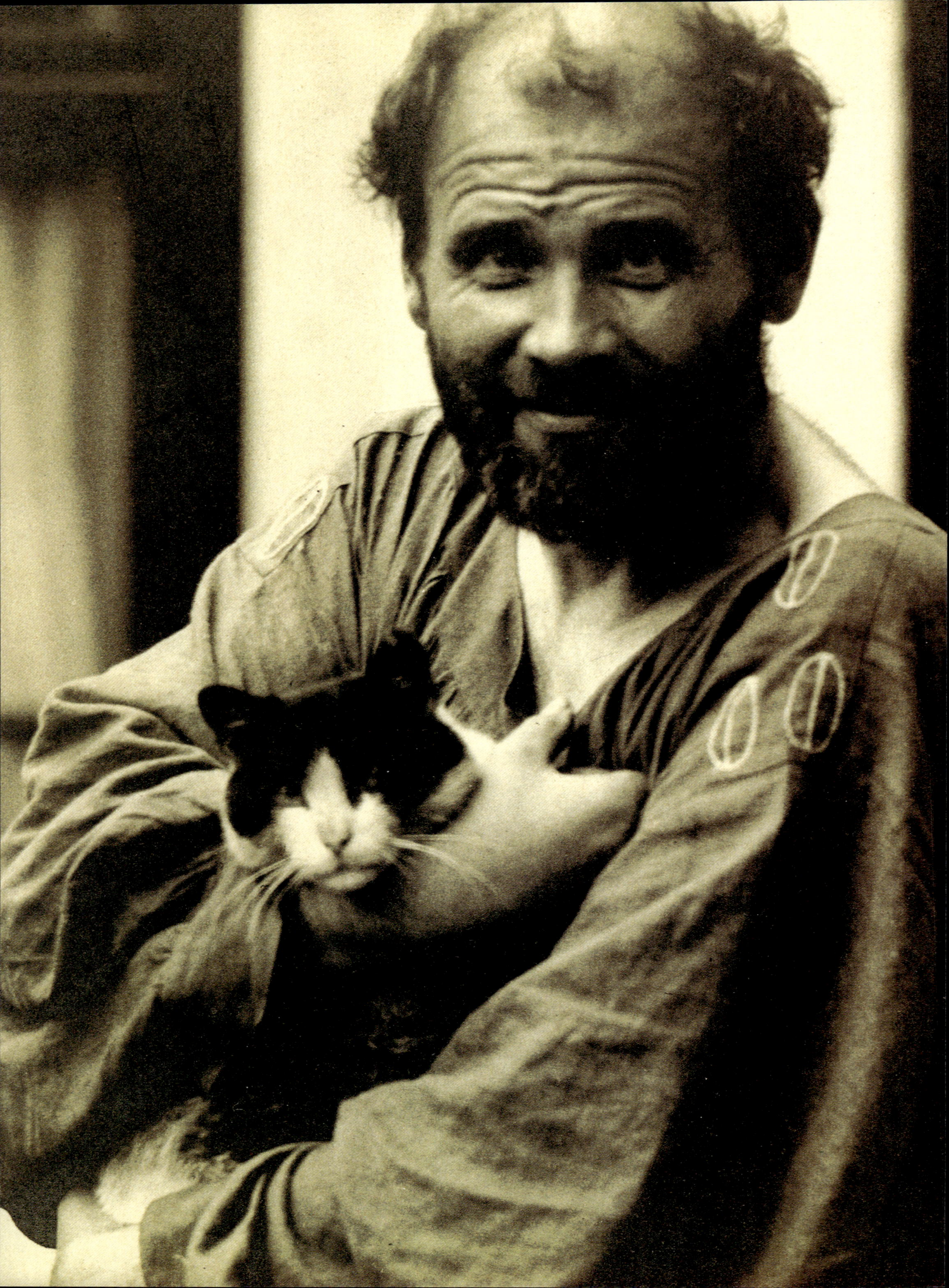

My whole life is waiting for the questions to which I have prepared answers.

Tom Stoppard

I do not mind lying, but I hate inaccuracy.

Samuel Butler

Her clothes have no buttons. There are two missing from my jacket. This lady and I are almost of the same religion.

Guillaume Apollinaire

An ideal map would contain the map of the map, the map of the map of the map … endlessly.

Alfred Korzybski

Since we are destined to live out our lives in the prison of our minds, our one duty is to furnish it well.

Peter Ustinov

Basic research is what I am doing when I don't know what I am doing.

Werner Von Braun

I've always loved the back of your neck, the only part of you I could look at without being seen.

Henri-Pierre Rouché

It requires a very unusual mind to undertake the analysis of the obvious.

Alfred North Whitehead

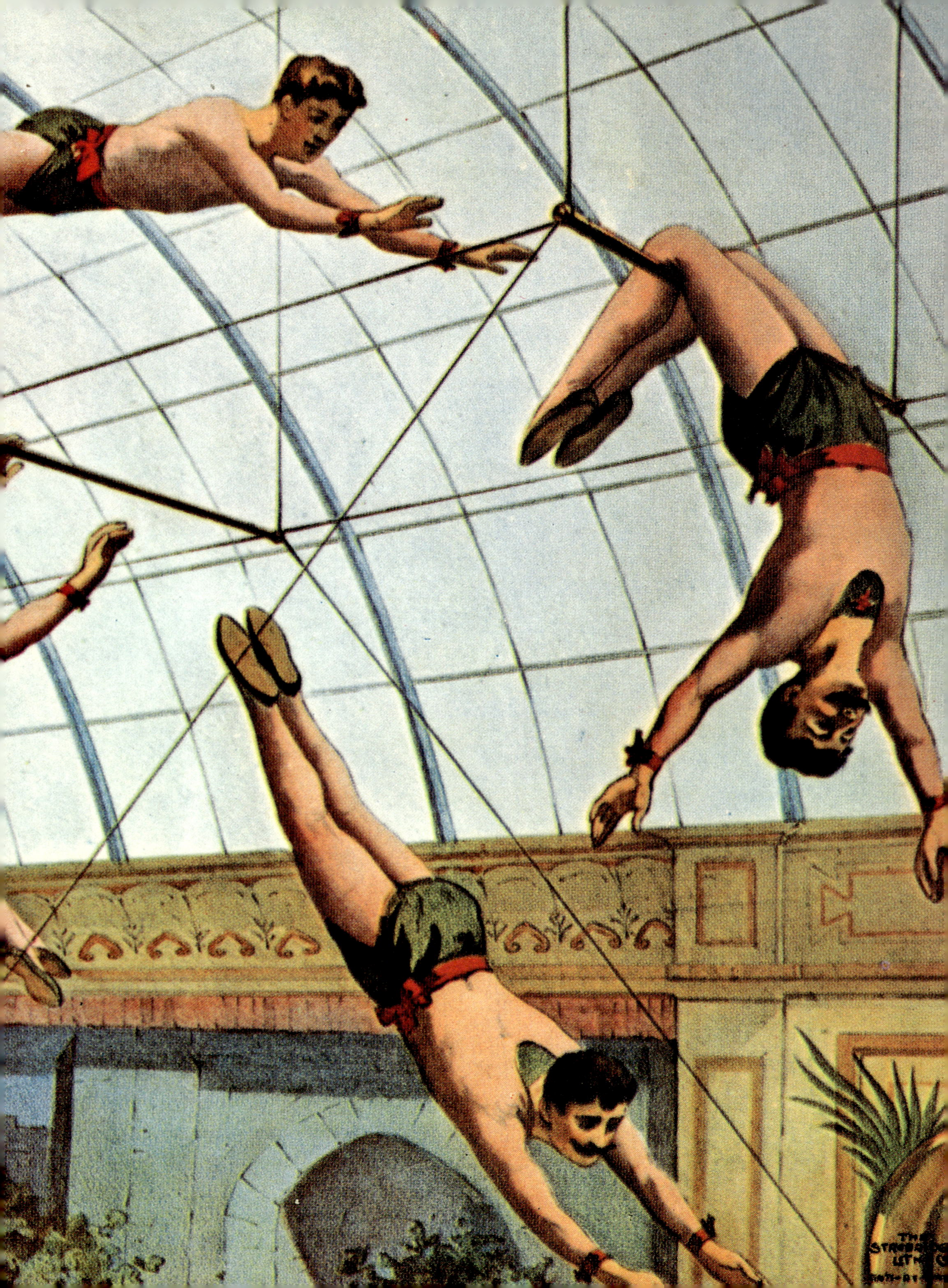

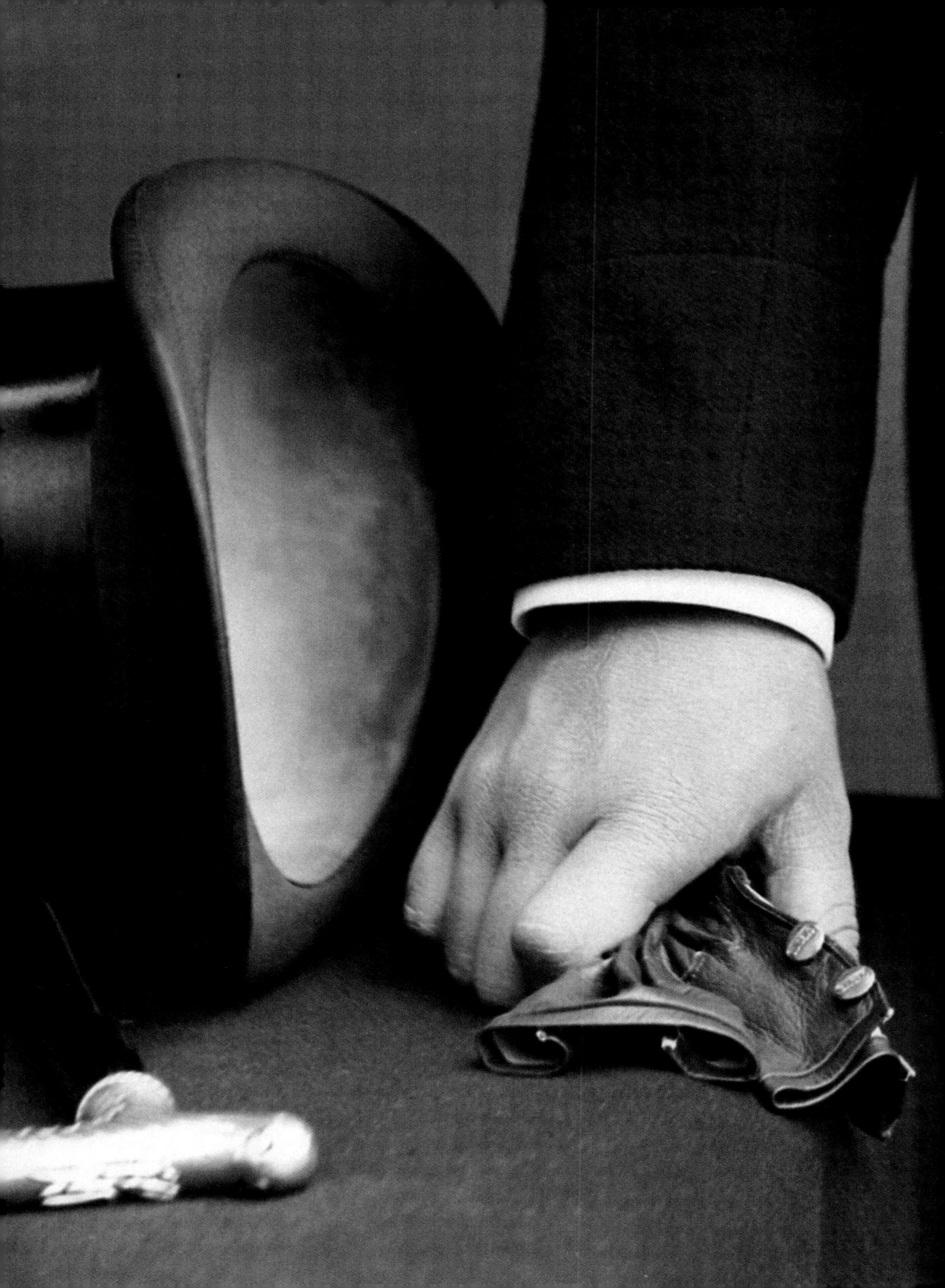

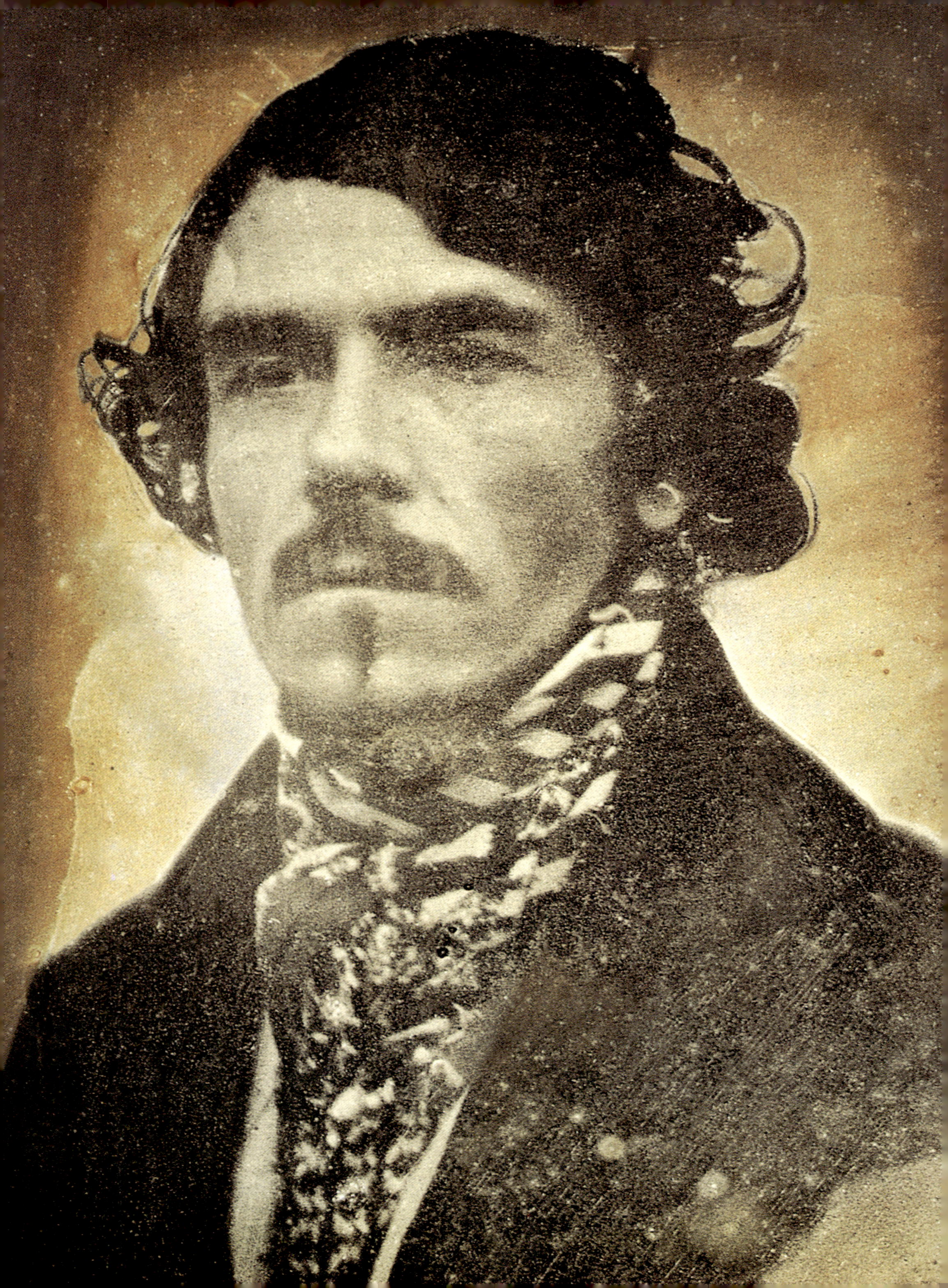

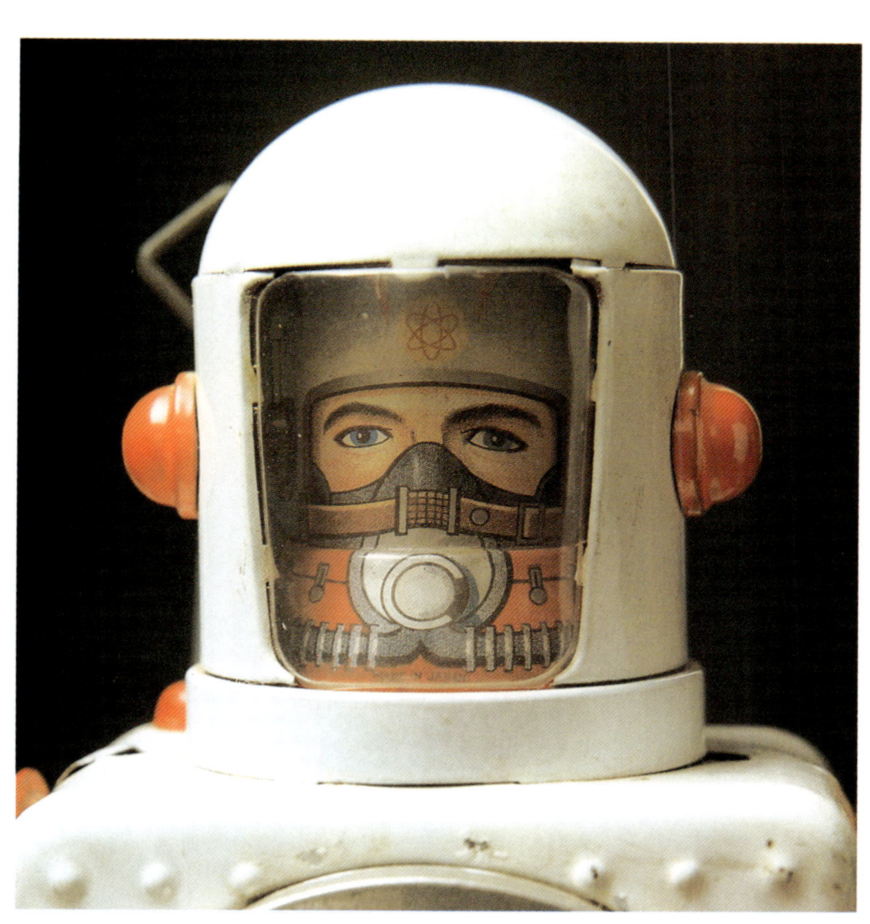

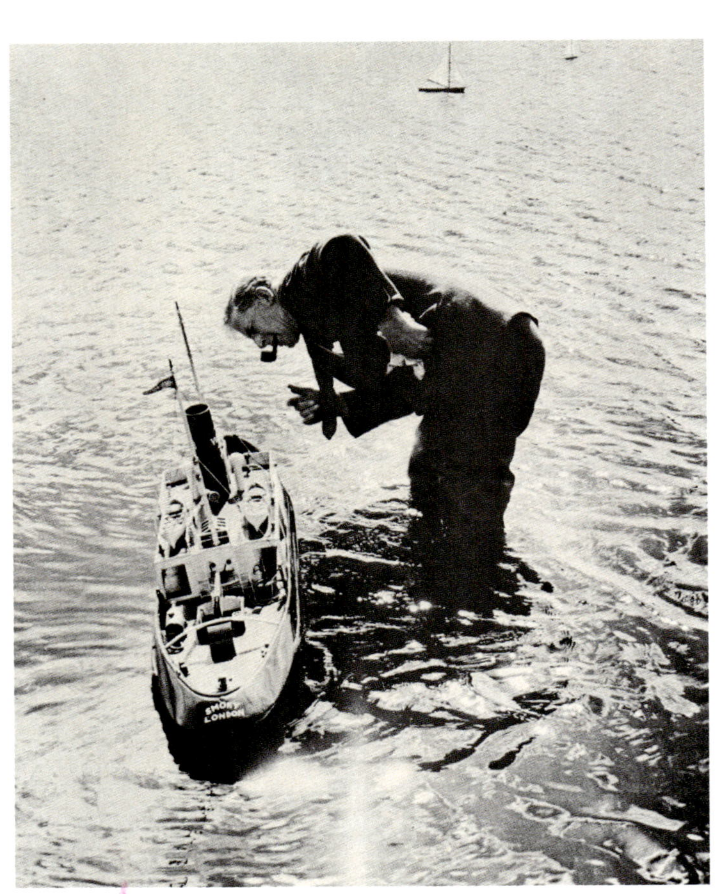

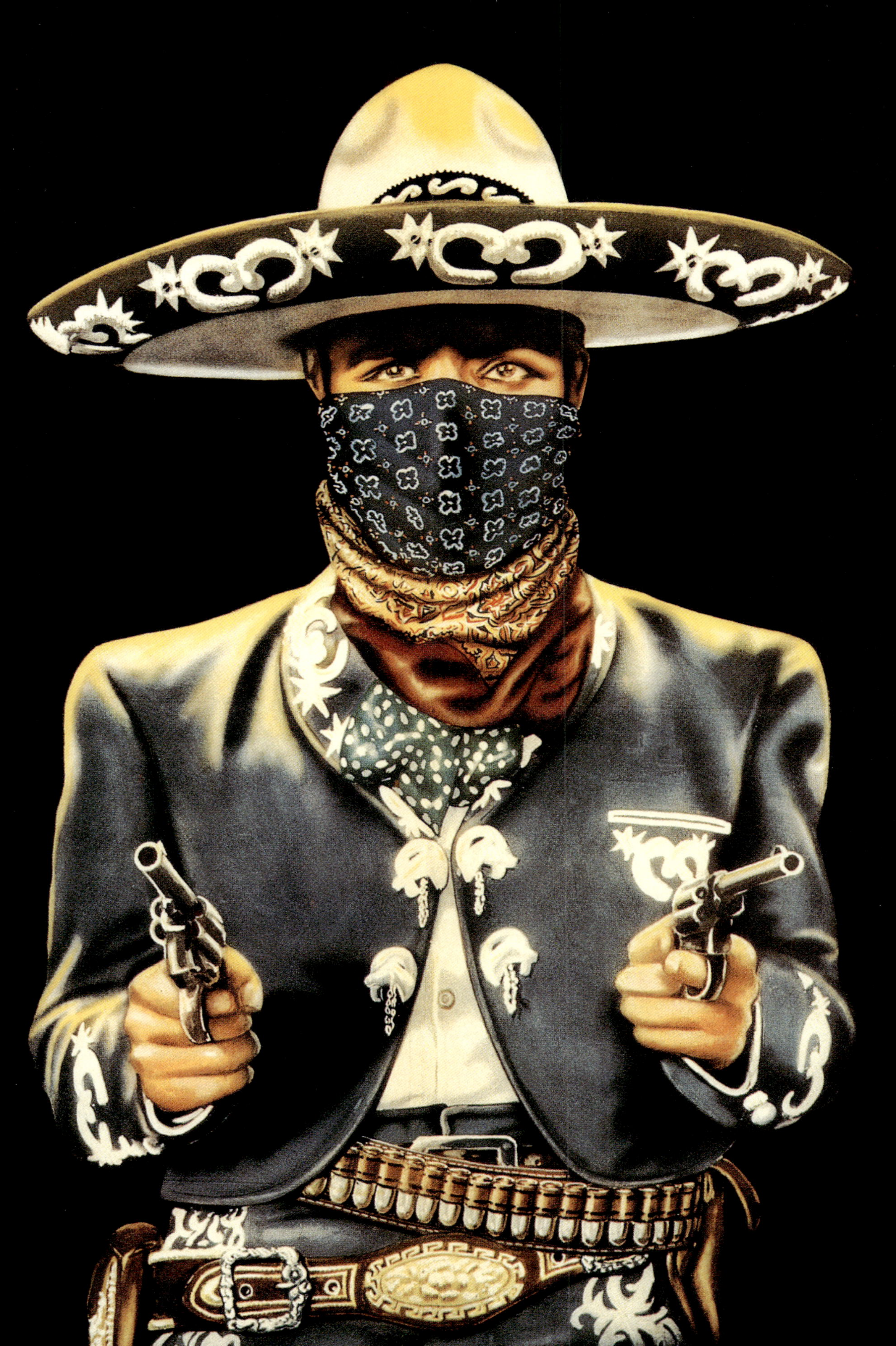

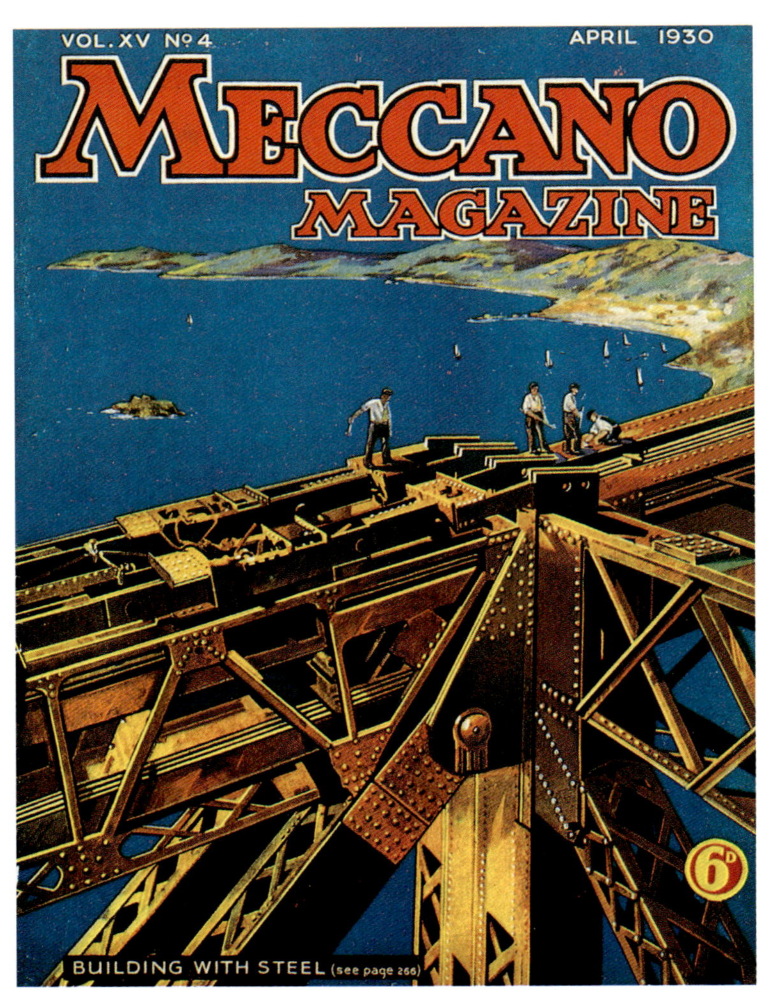

VOL. XV Nº 4
APRIL 1930
MECCANO
MAGAZINE
6D
BUILDING WITH STEEL (see page 266)

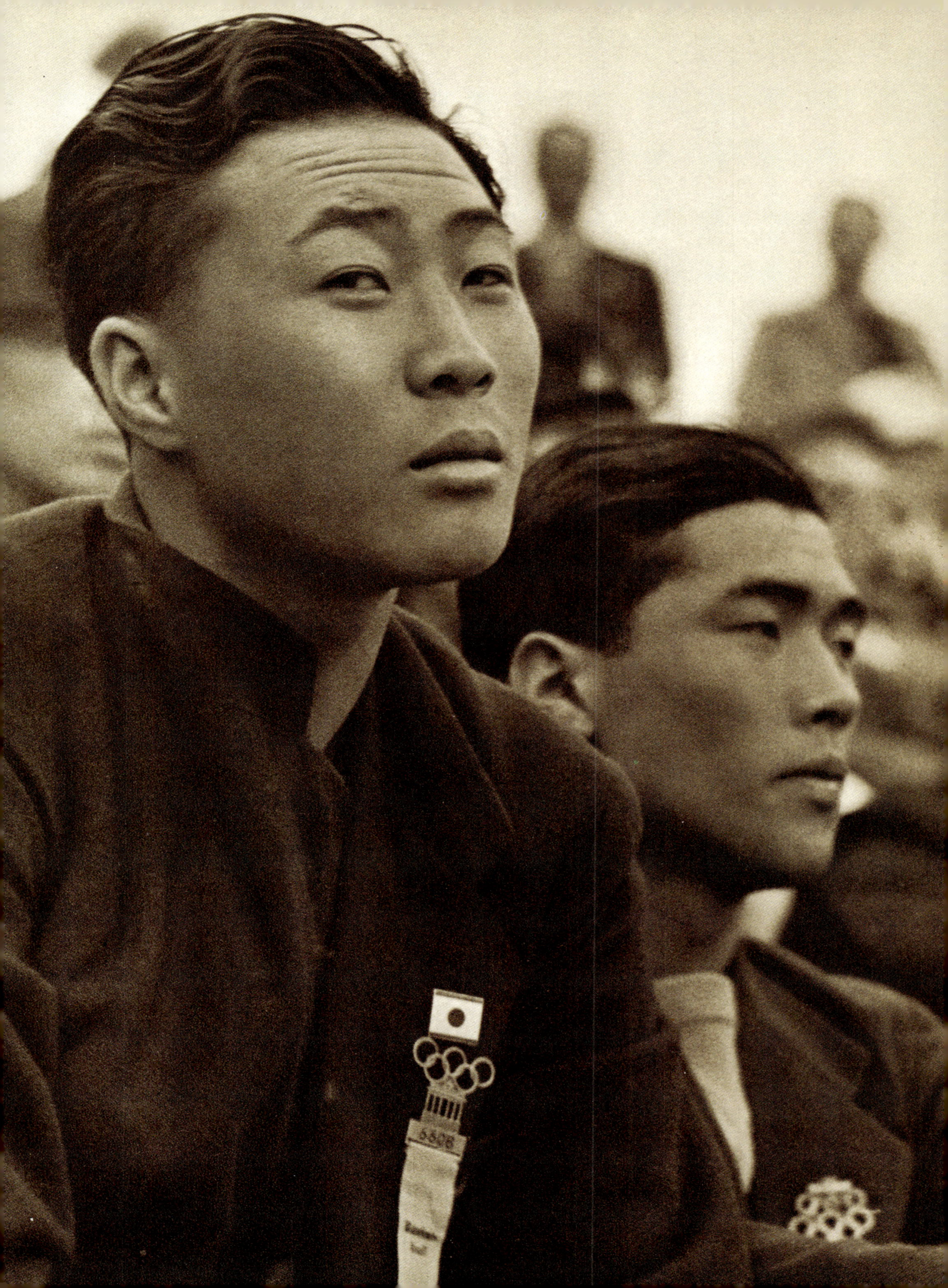

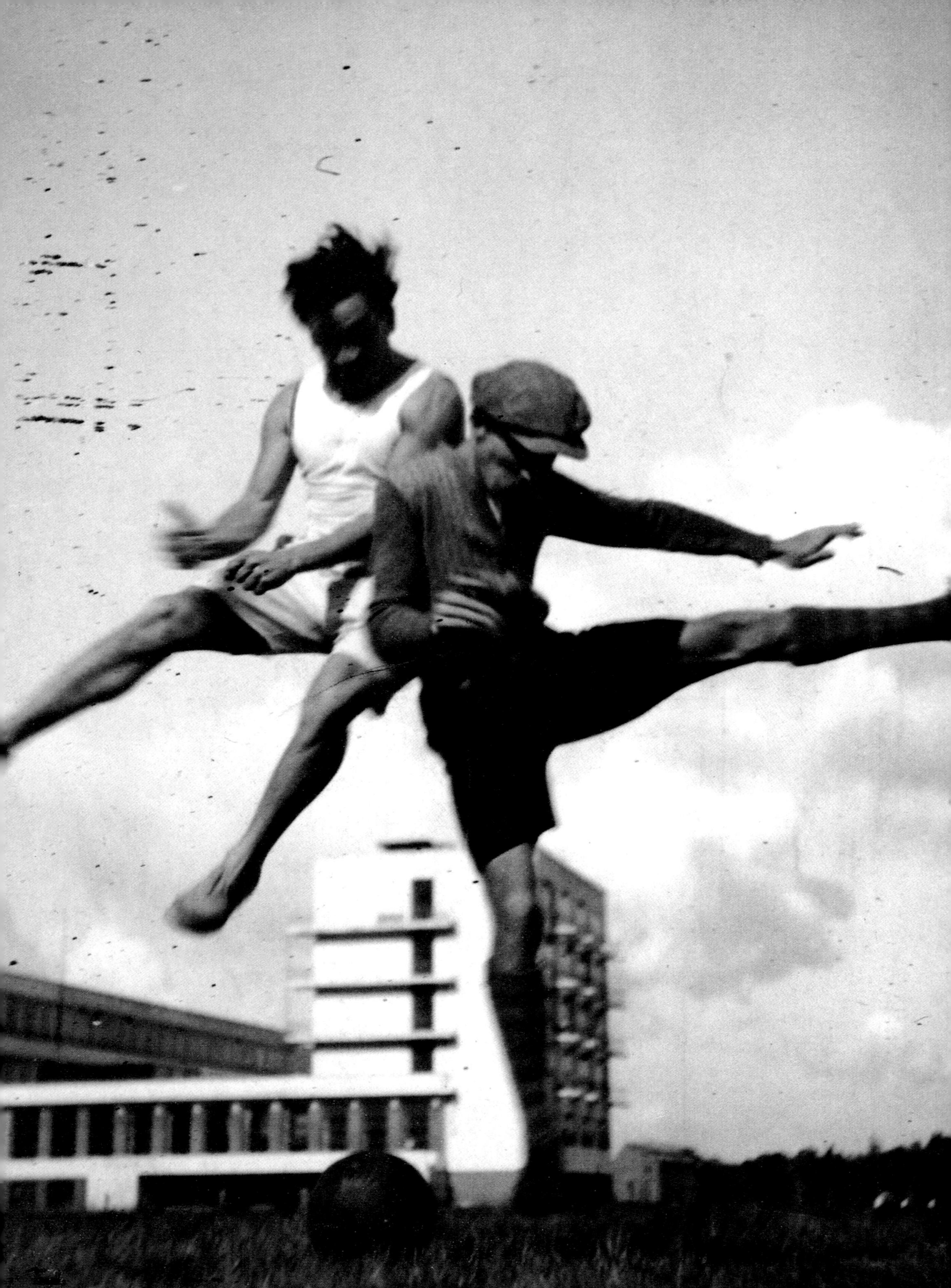

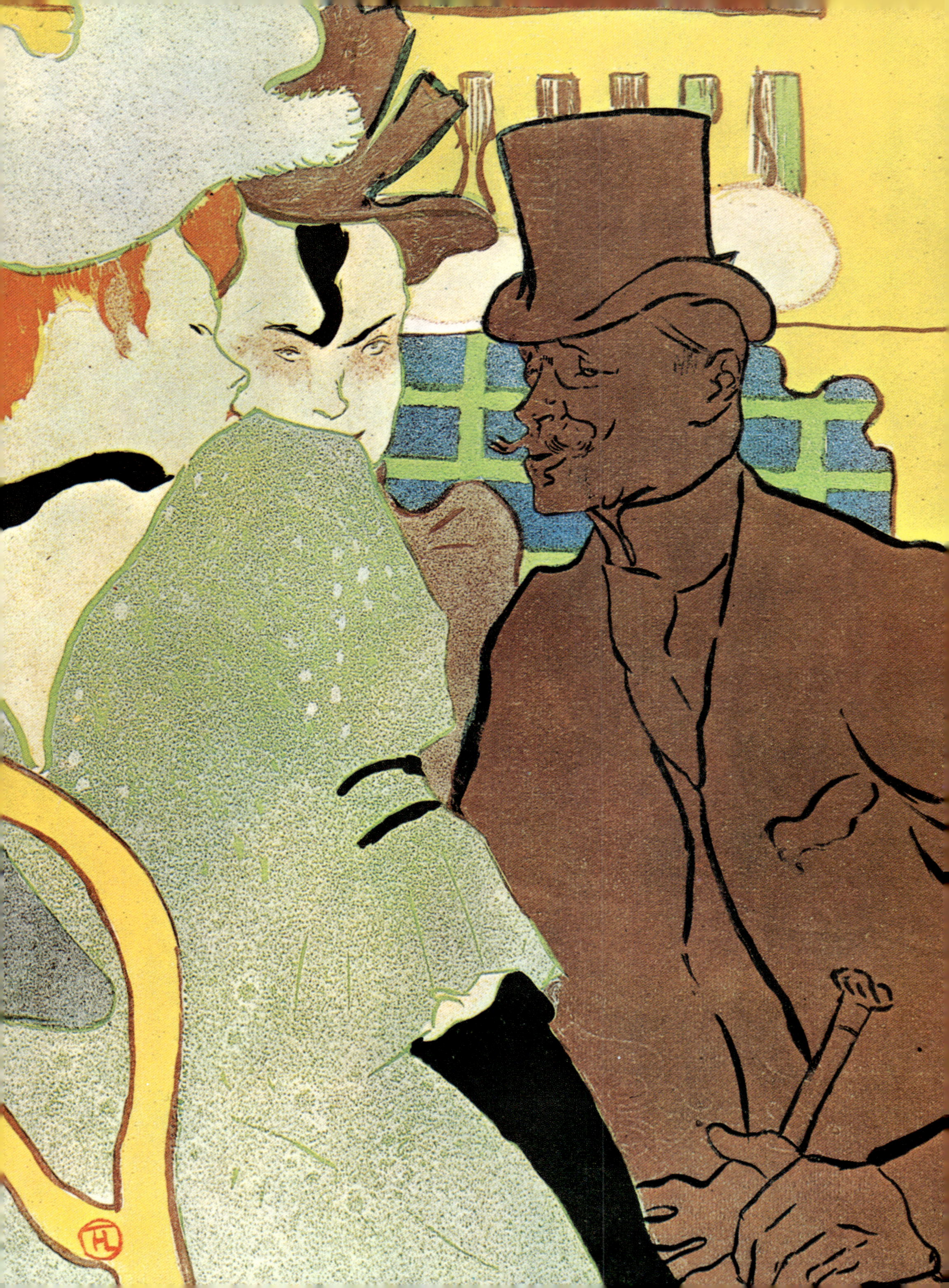

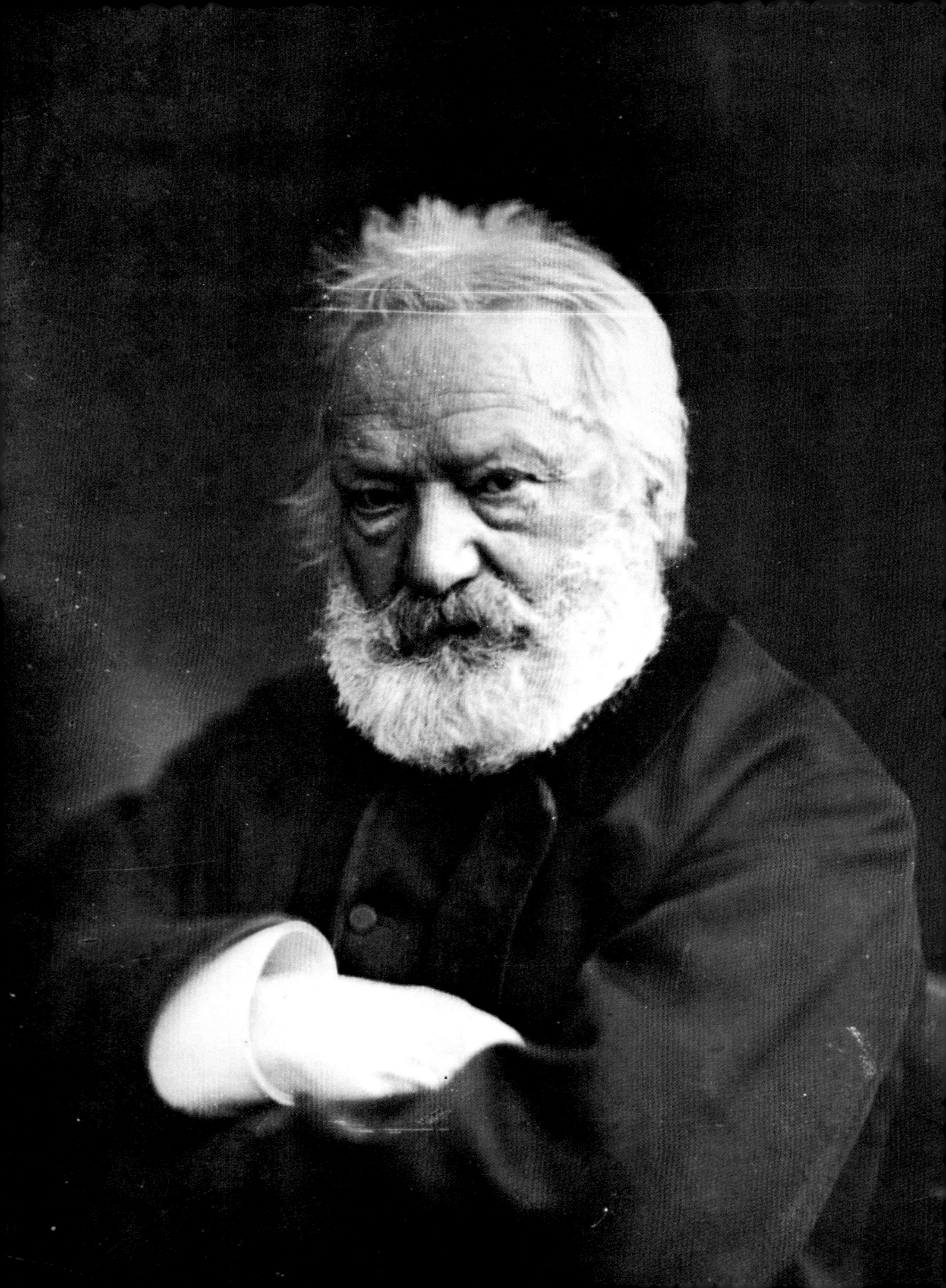

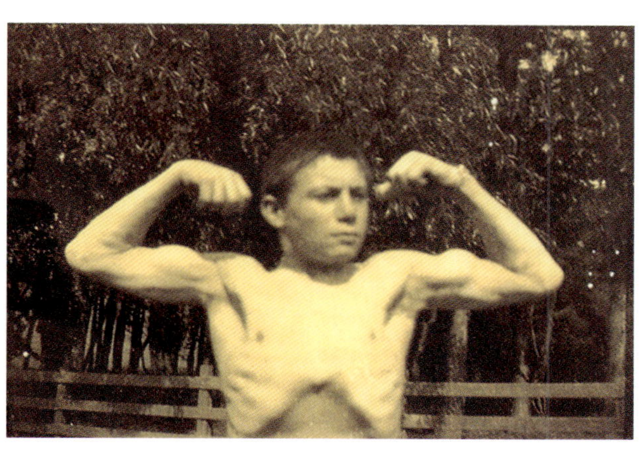

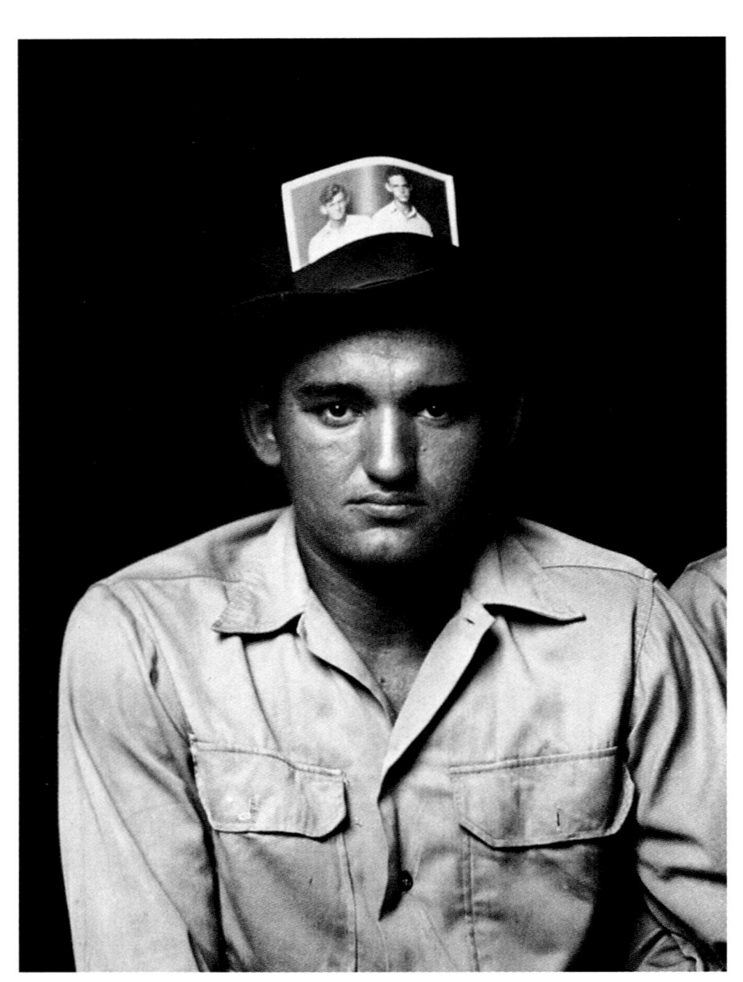

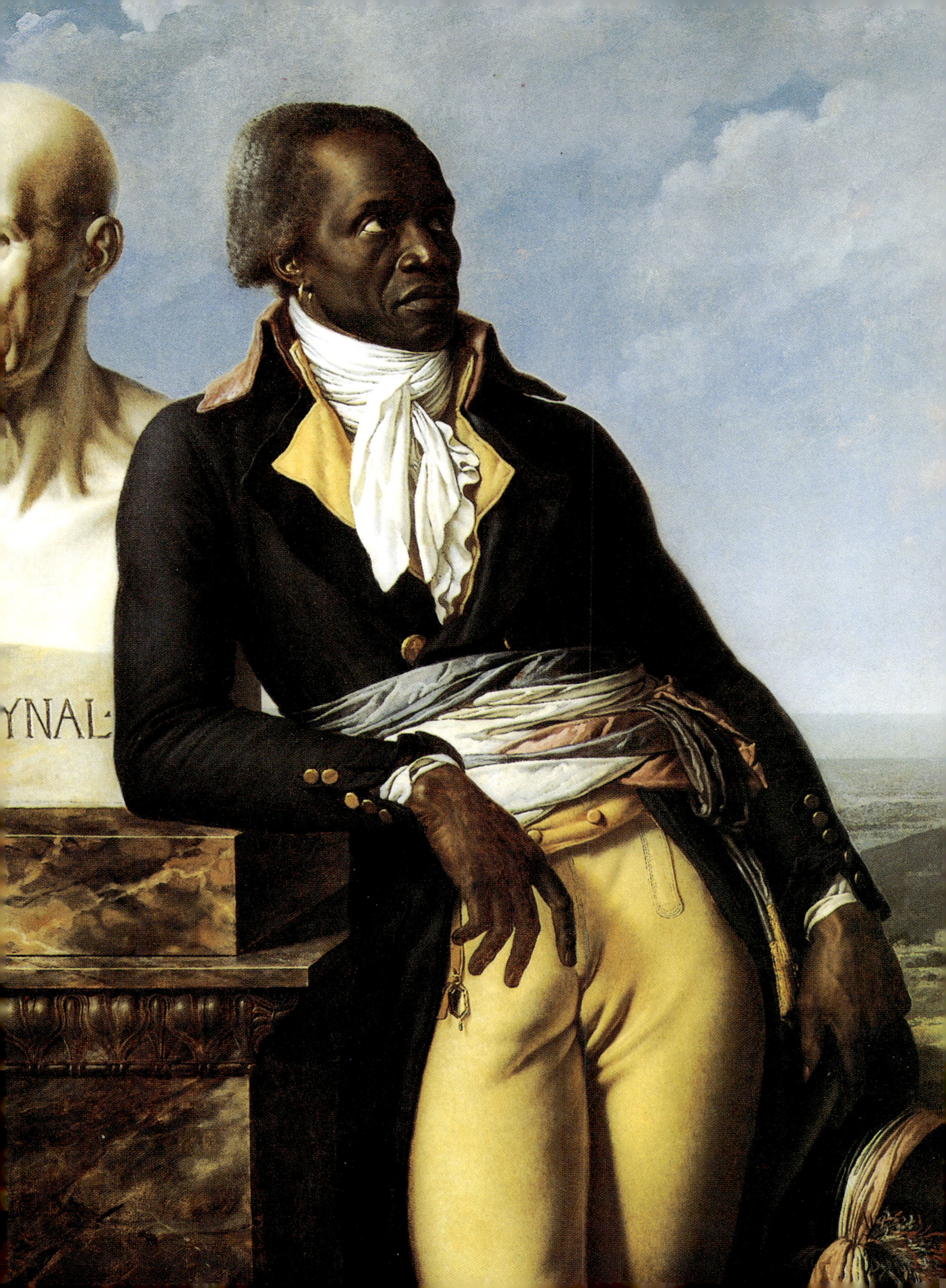
YNAL

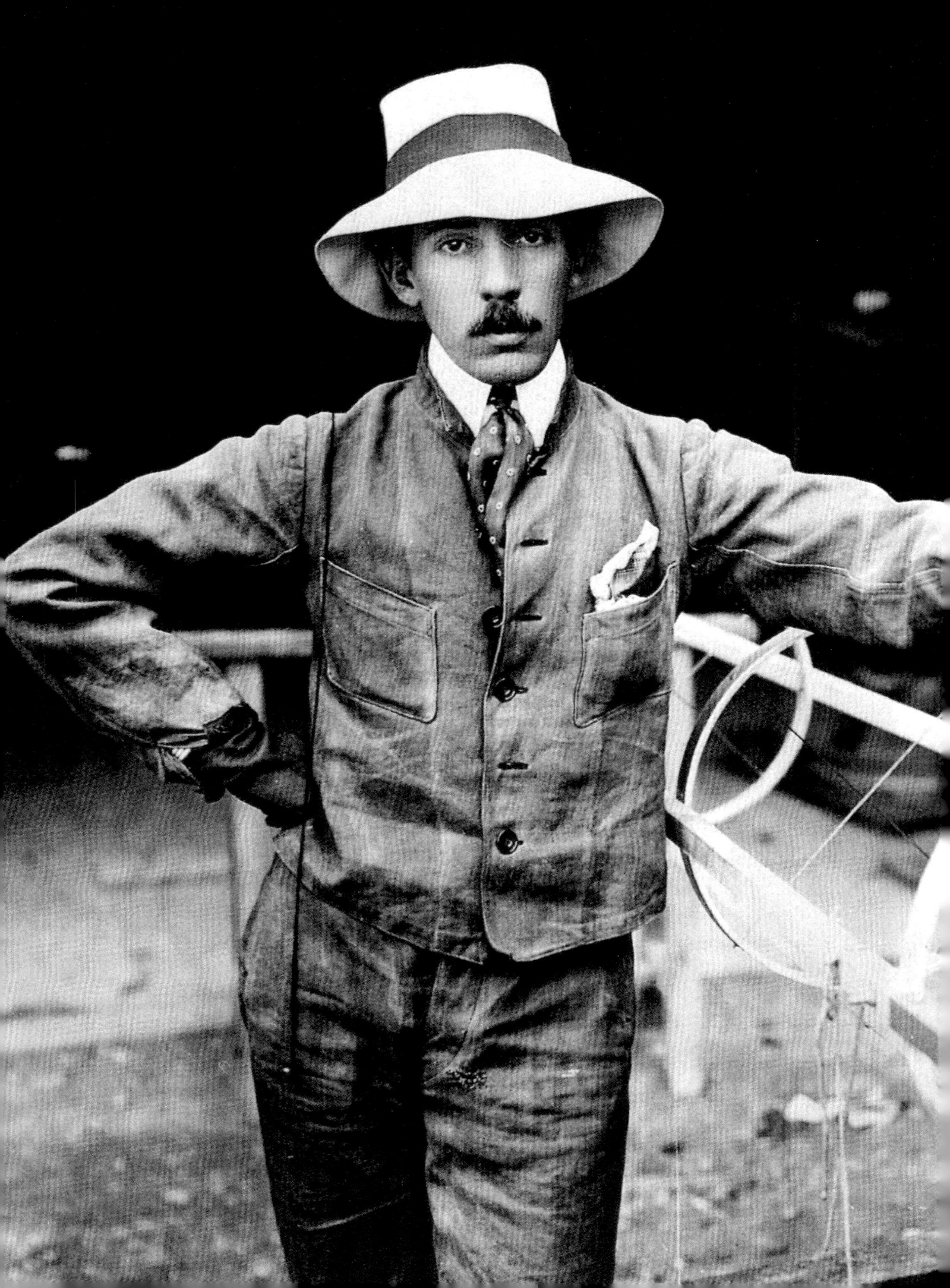

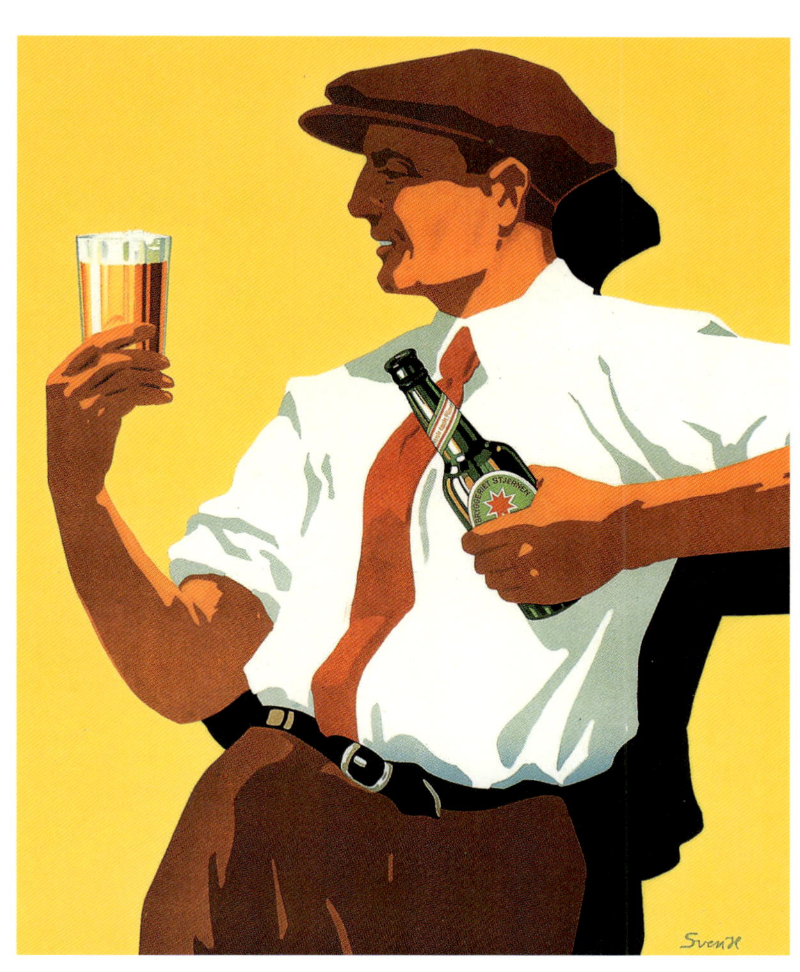
BRYGGERIET STJERNEN
SvenH

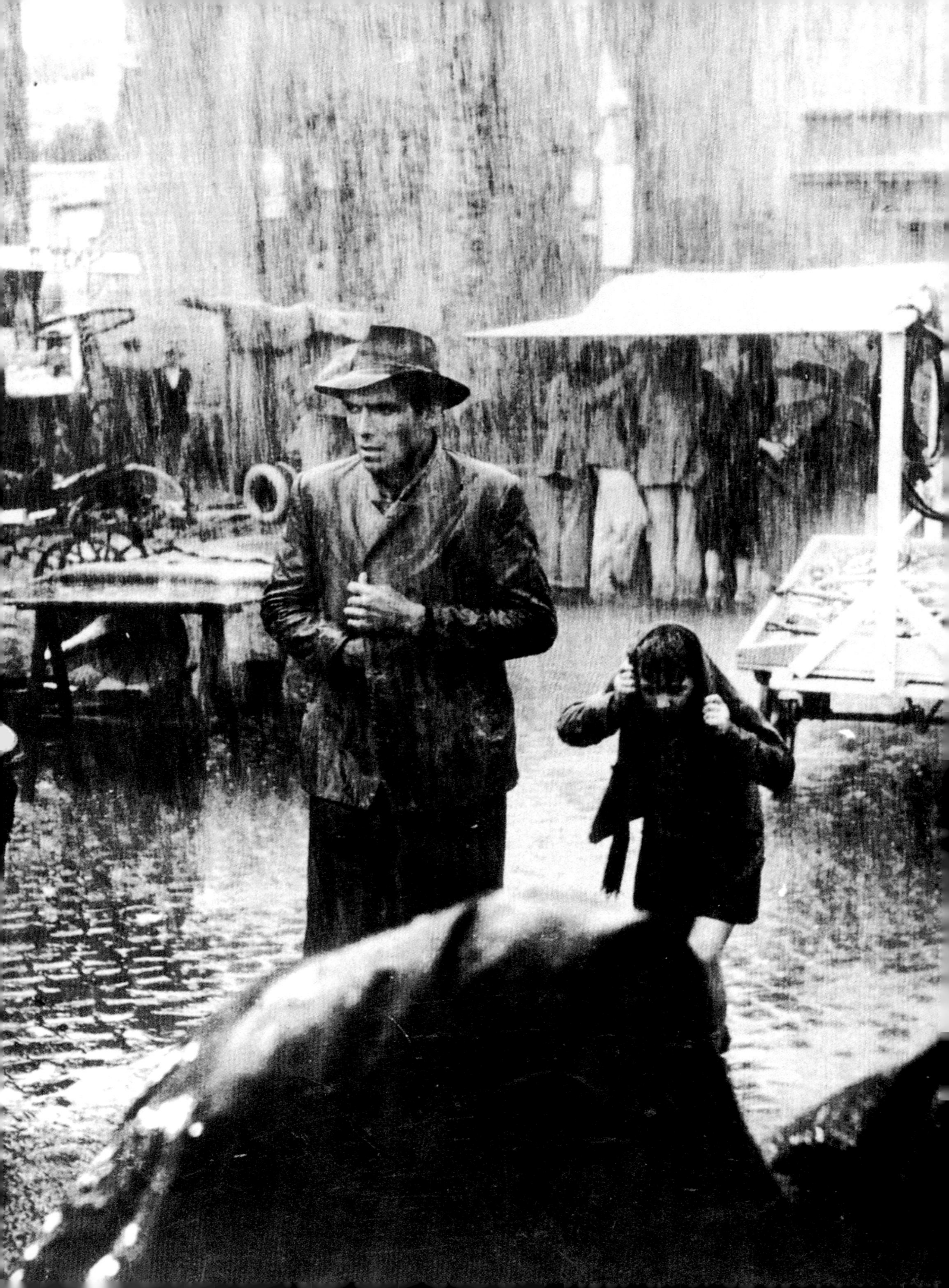

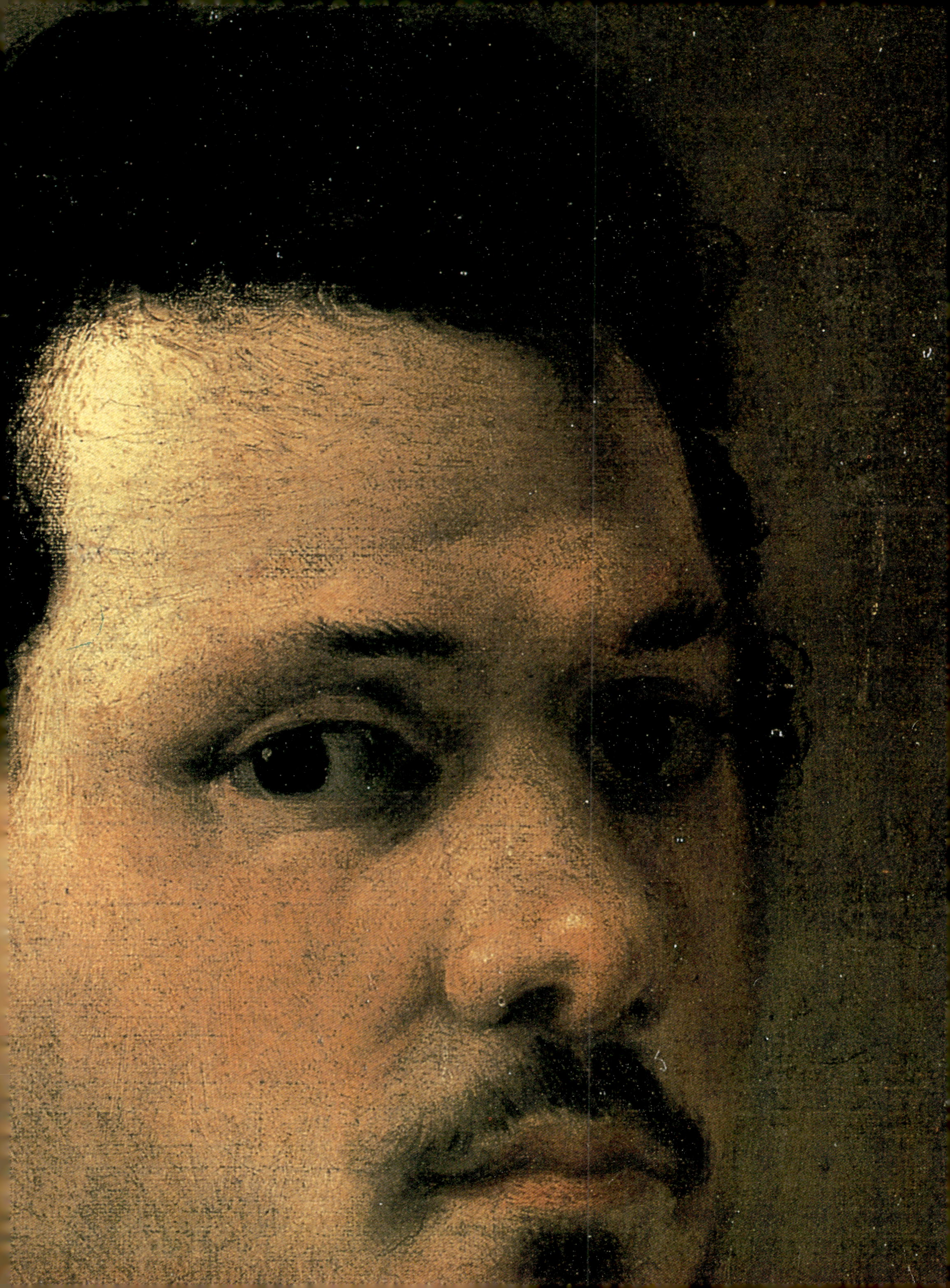

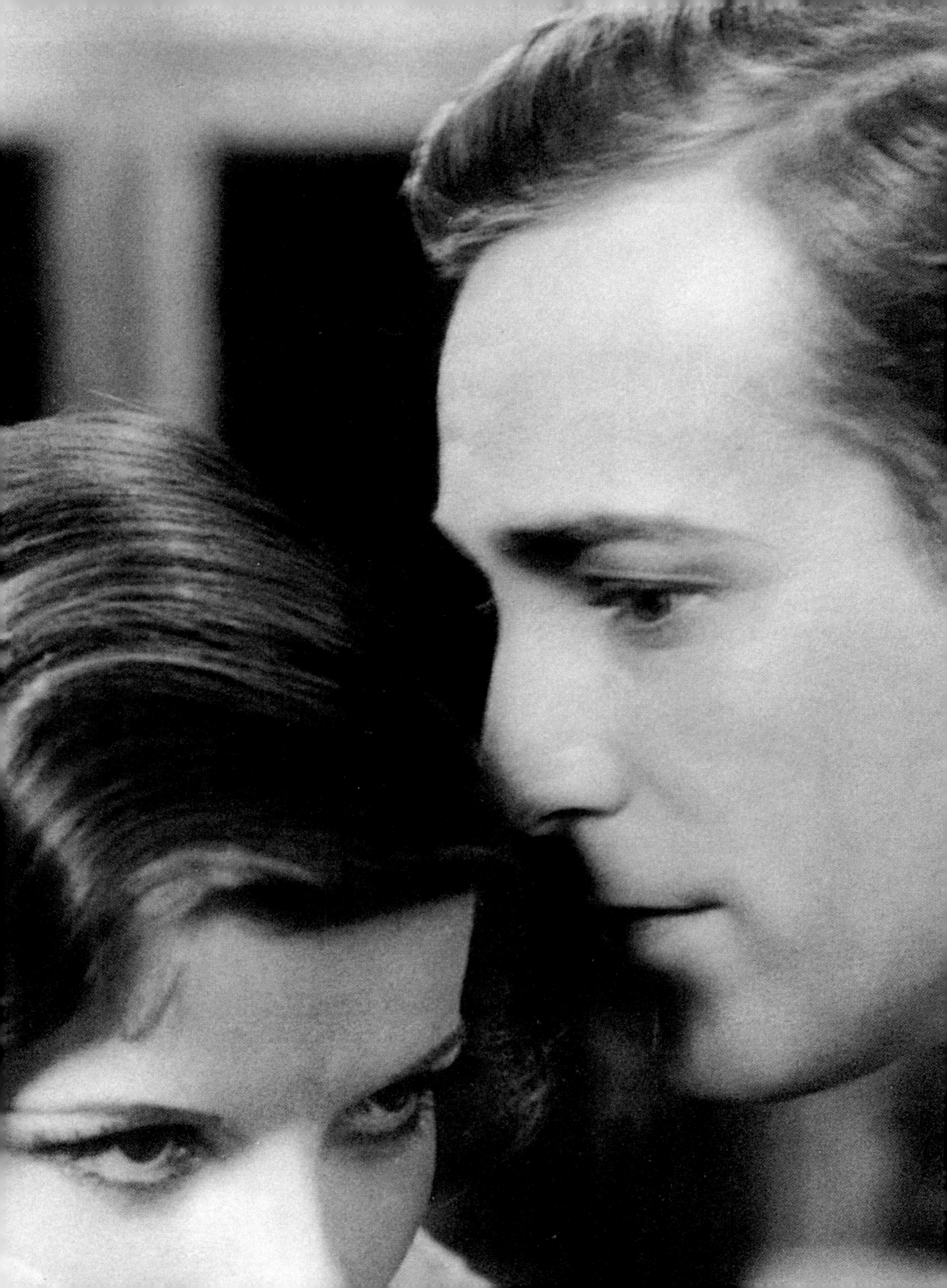

More than love, my father knew how to bear love.

James Wright

We are happy when for everything inside us there is a corresponding something outside us.

William Butler Yeats

My mind has been in control all of my life and it would kill me rather than relinquish control.

Carlos Castaneda

I carefully number the bricks of my heart for a later reconstruction.

Jeff Silva

That's how it goes, my friend. The problem is not falling captive, it's how to avoid surrender.

Nazim Hikmet

Many a wave would rise on the past towards you; or else, perhaps, as you went by an open window, a violin would be giving itself to someone. All this was a trust. But were you equal to it? Were you not always distracted by expectation, as though all this were announcing someone to love?

Rainer Maria Rilke

Concentrate, don't embroider.

Spencer Tracy

Since we value – and madly overvalue – whatever is ordered, we tend to impute order to whatever we value.

Unknown

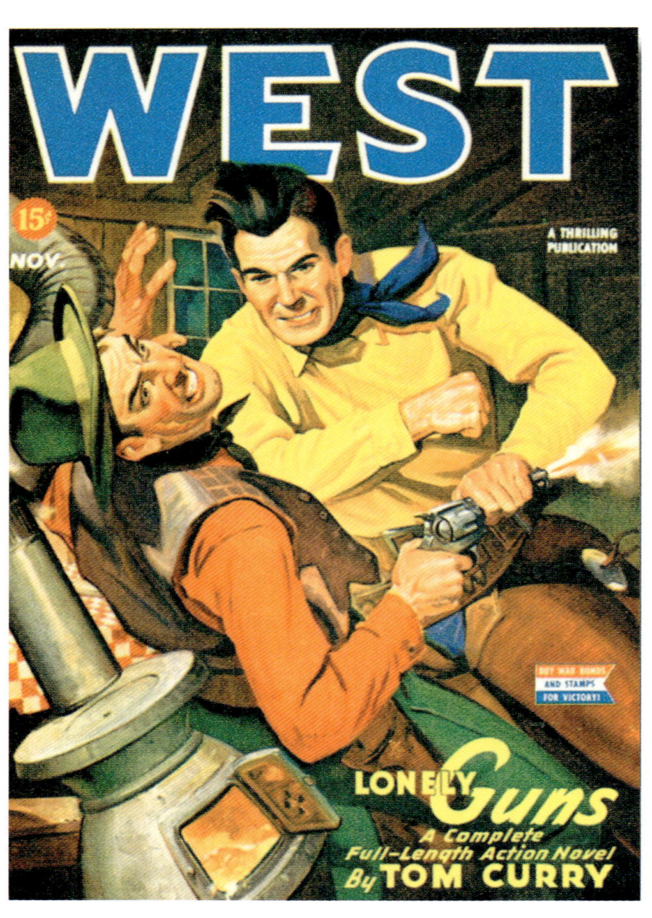

WEST
15¢
NOV.
A THRILLING PUBLICATION
BUY WAR BONDS AND STAMPS FOR VICTORY!
LONELY Guns
A Complete
Full-Length Action Novel
By TOM CURRY

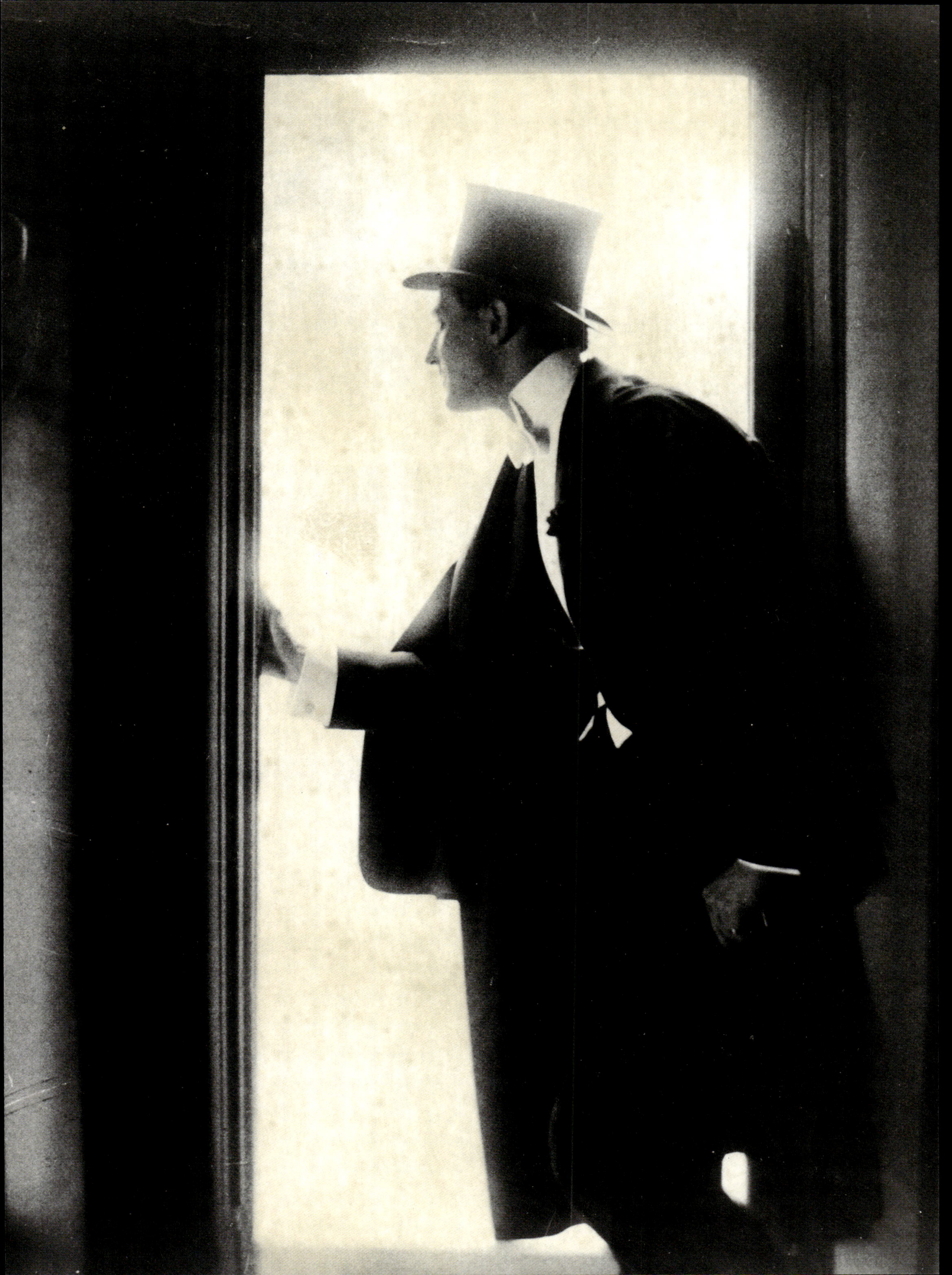

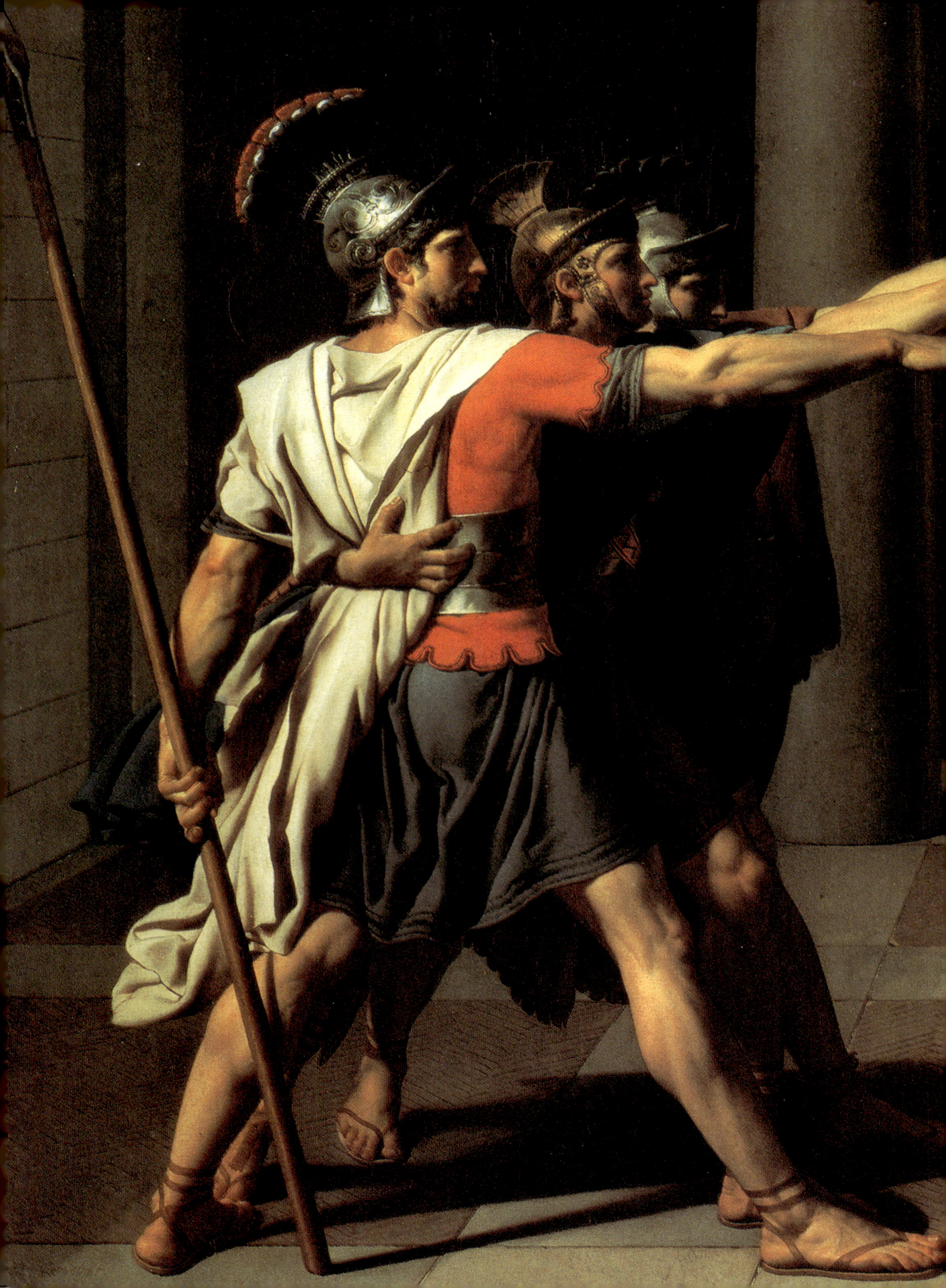

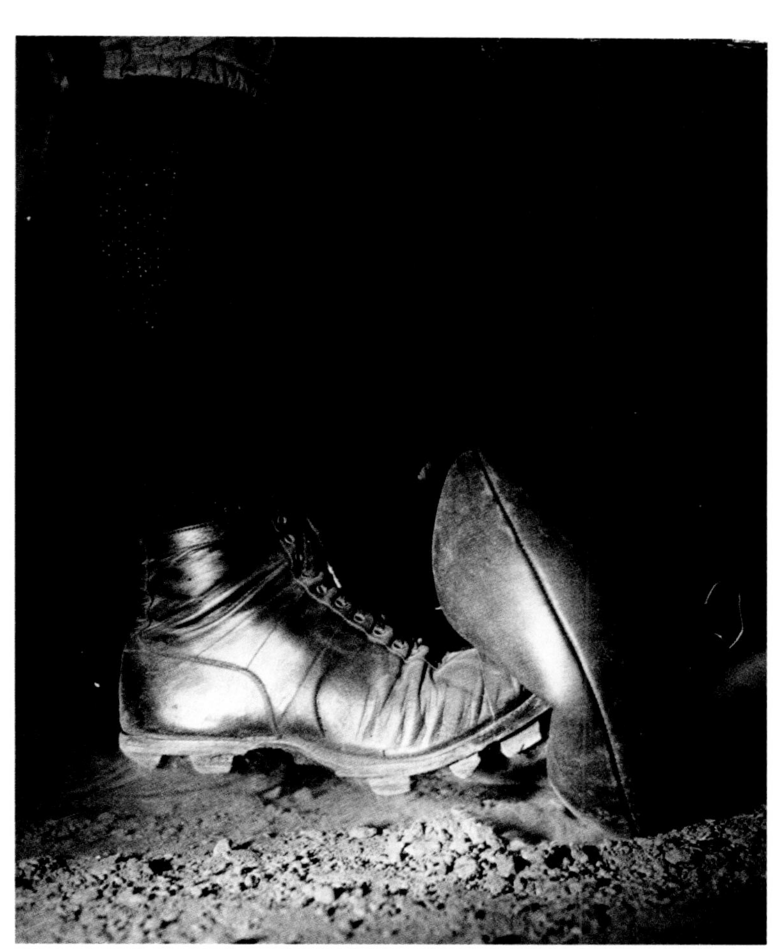

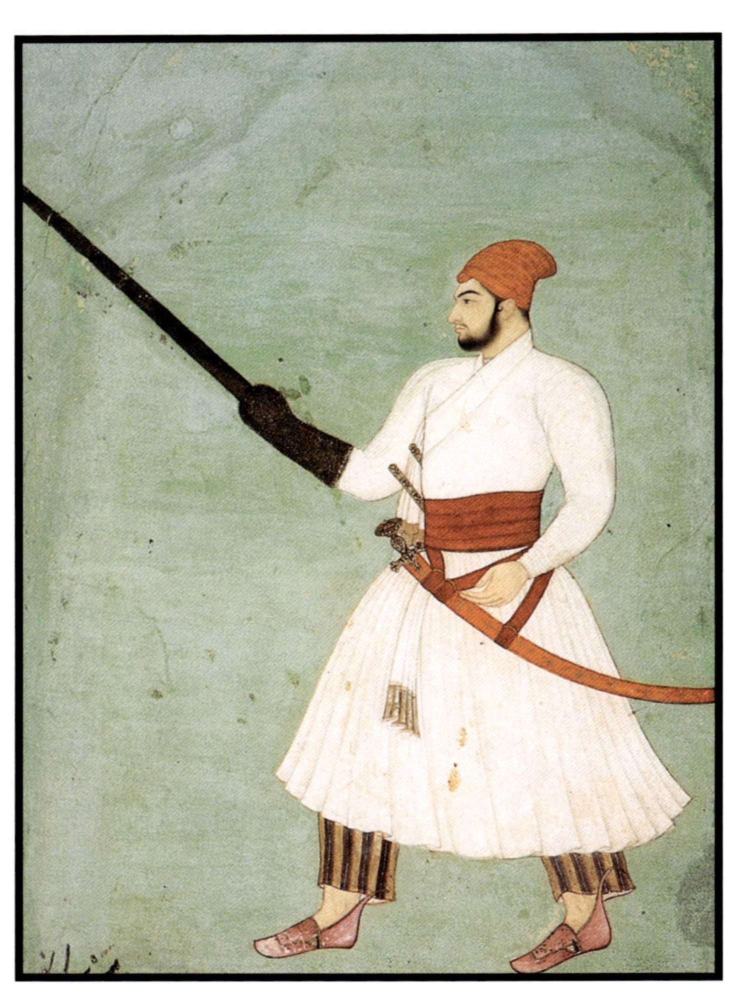

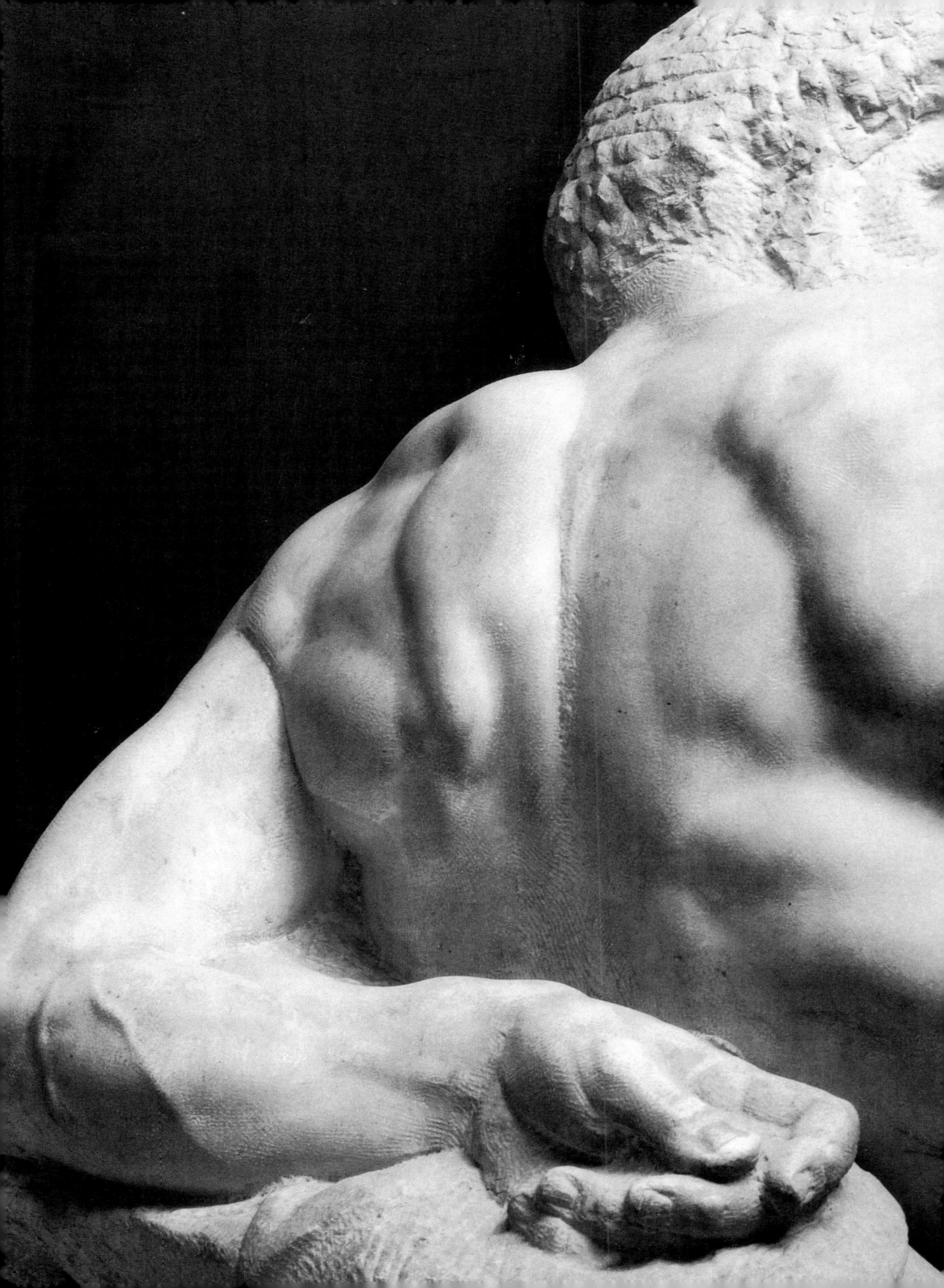

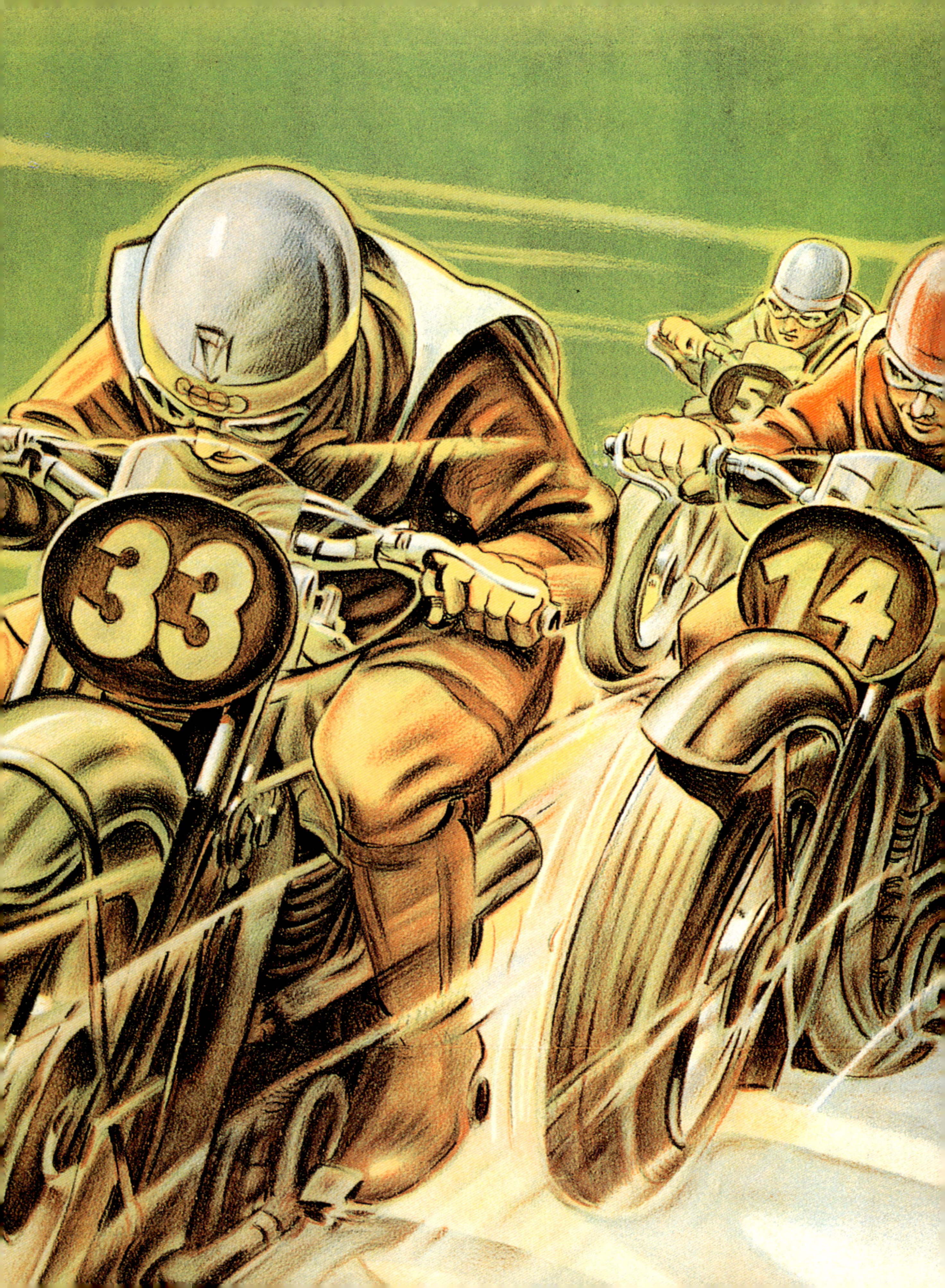

33
14

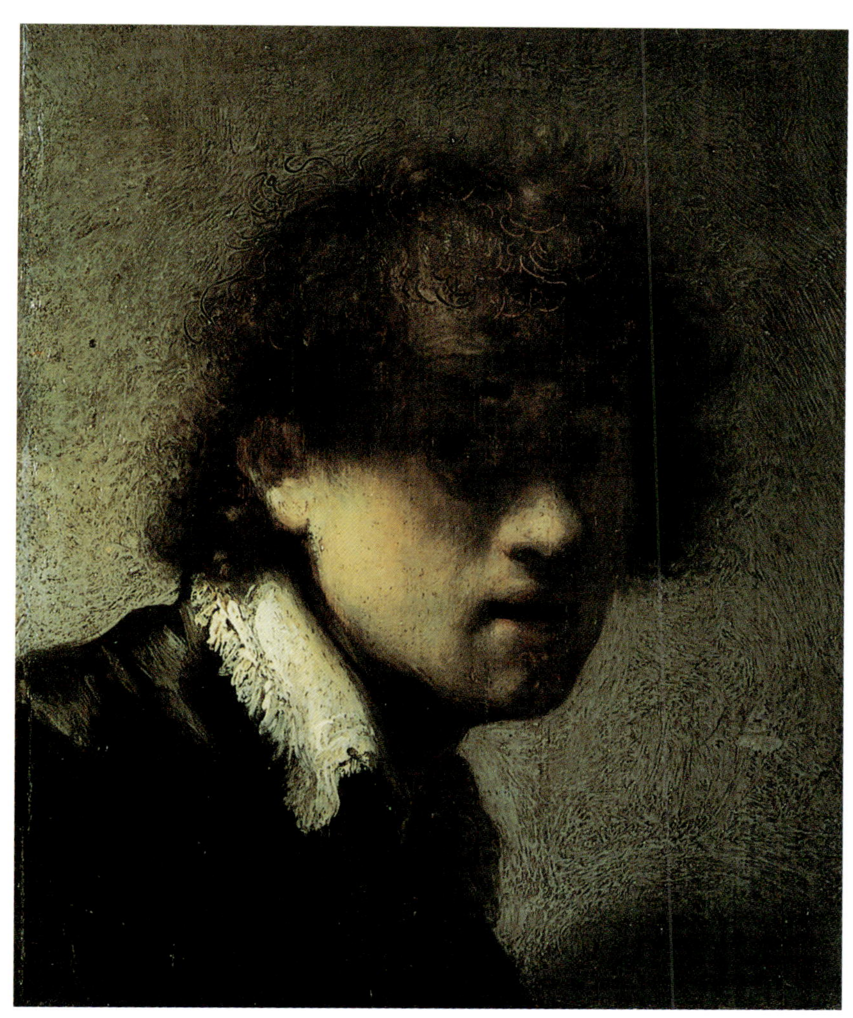

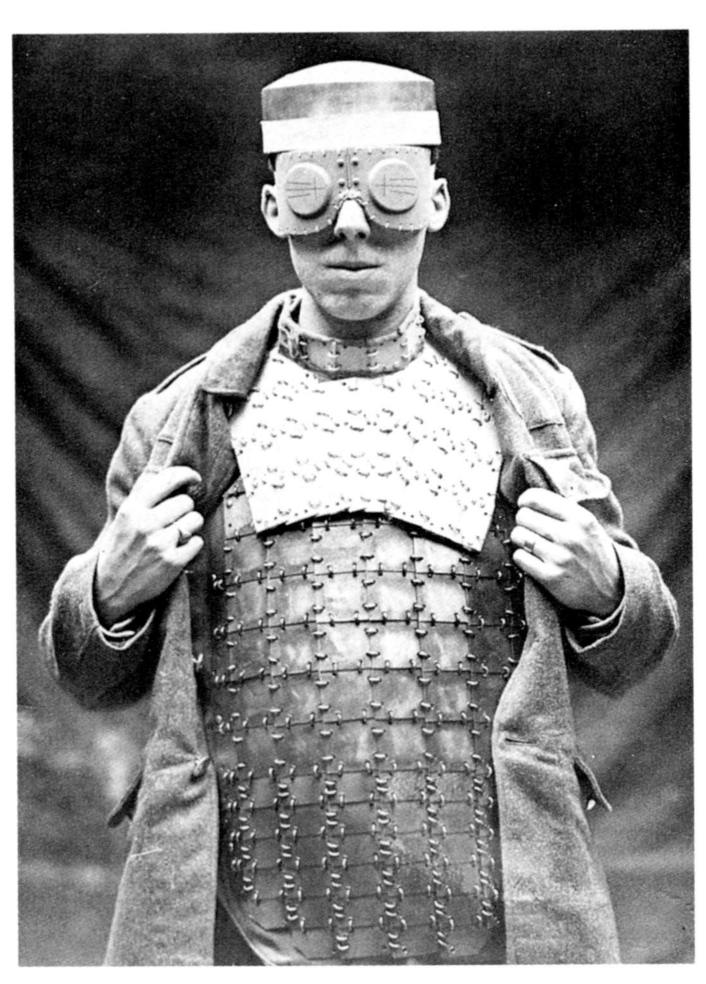

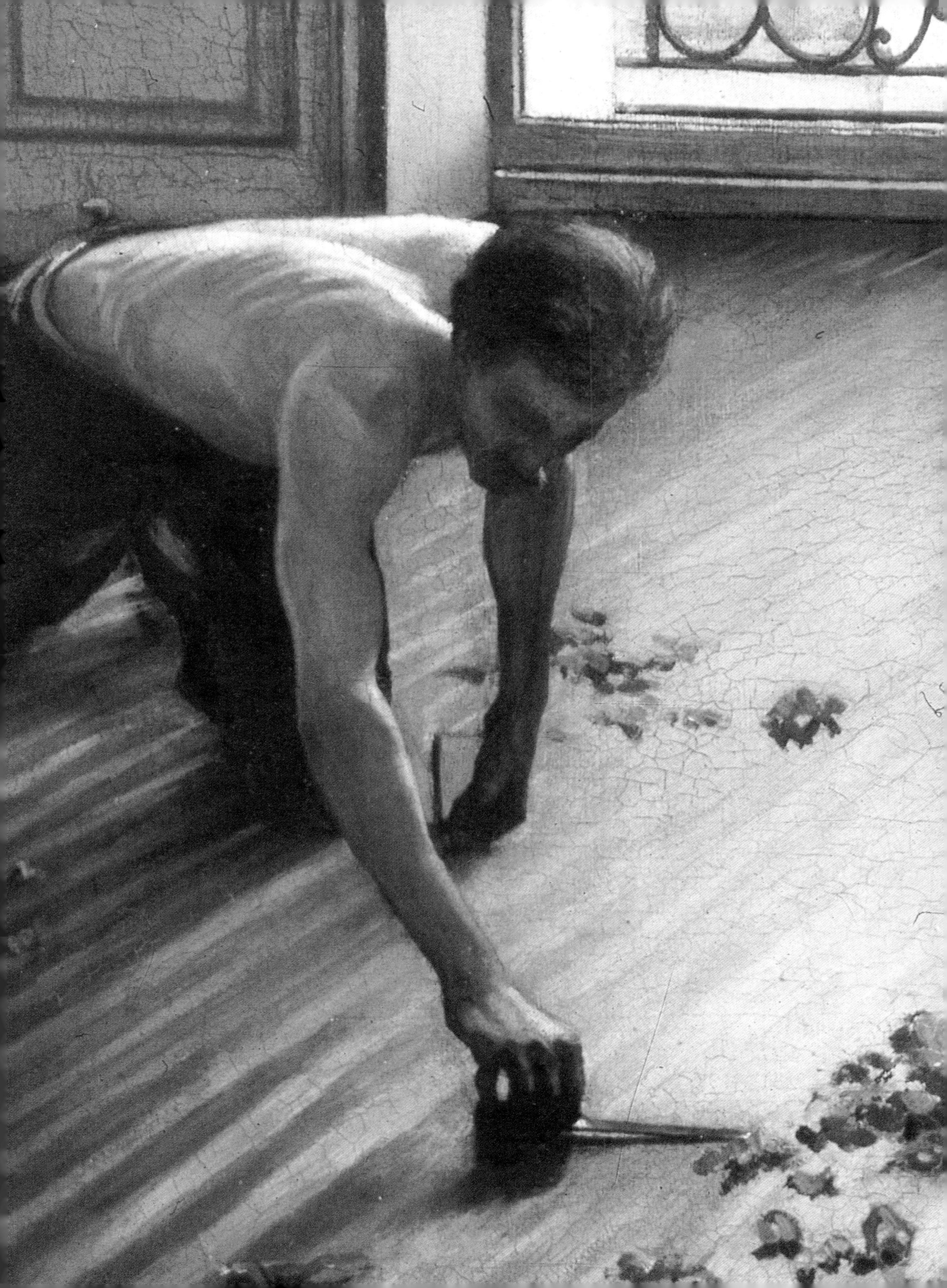

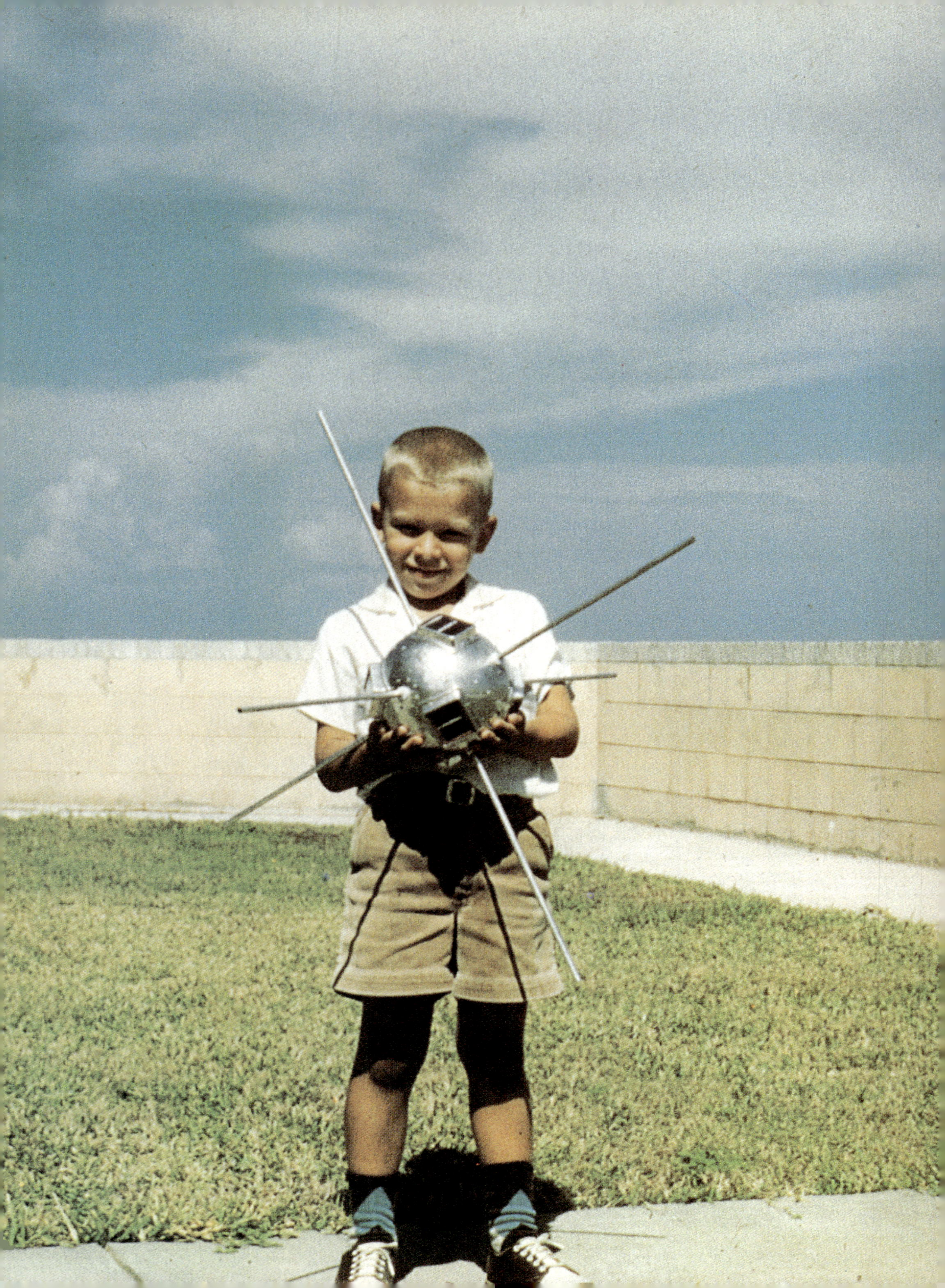

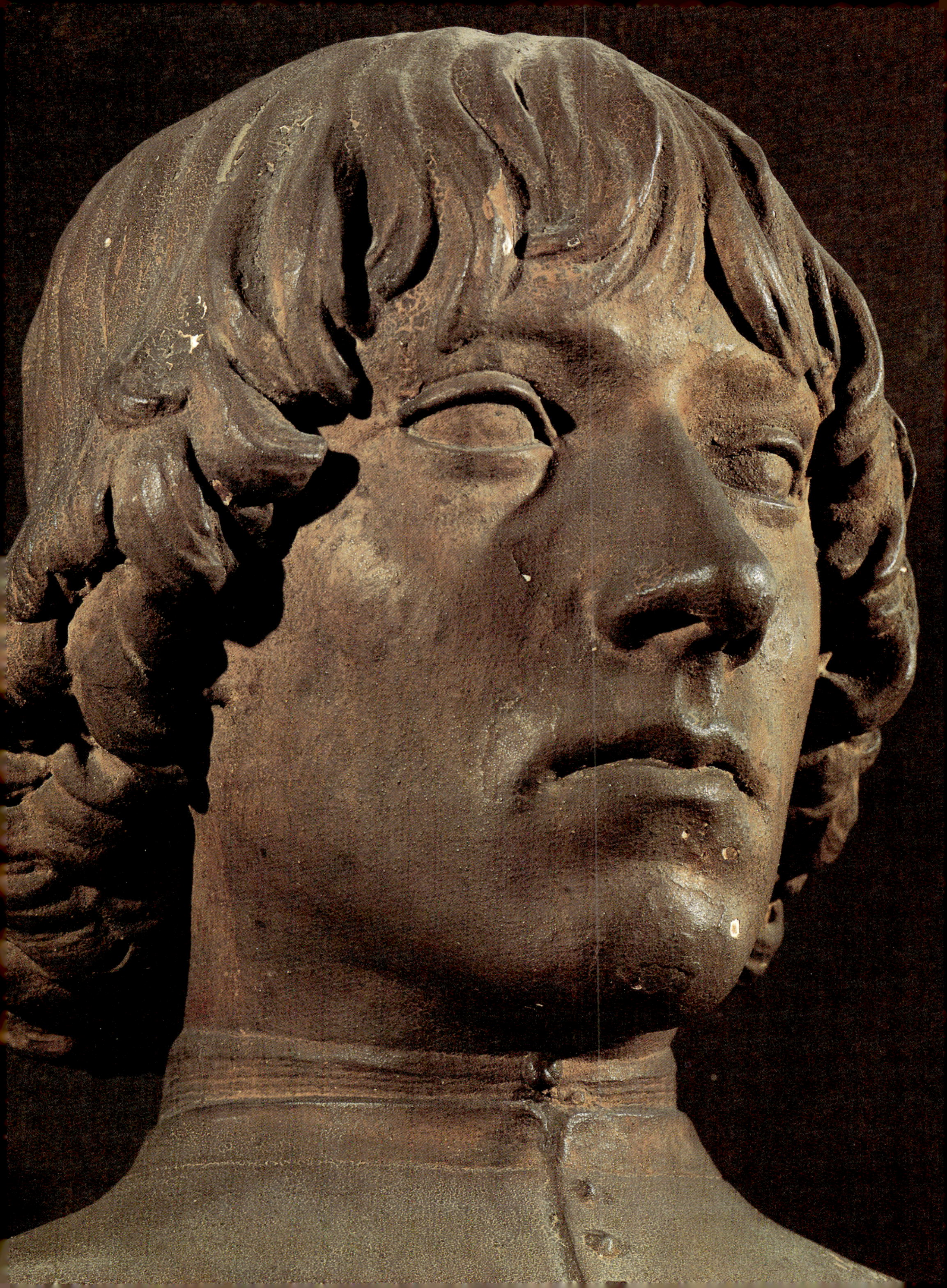

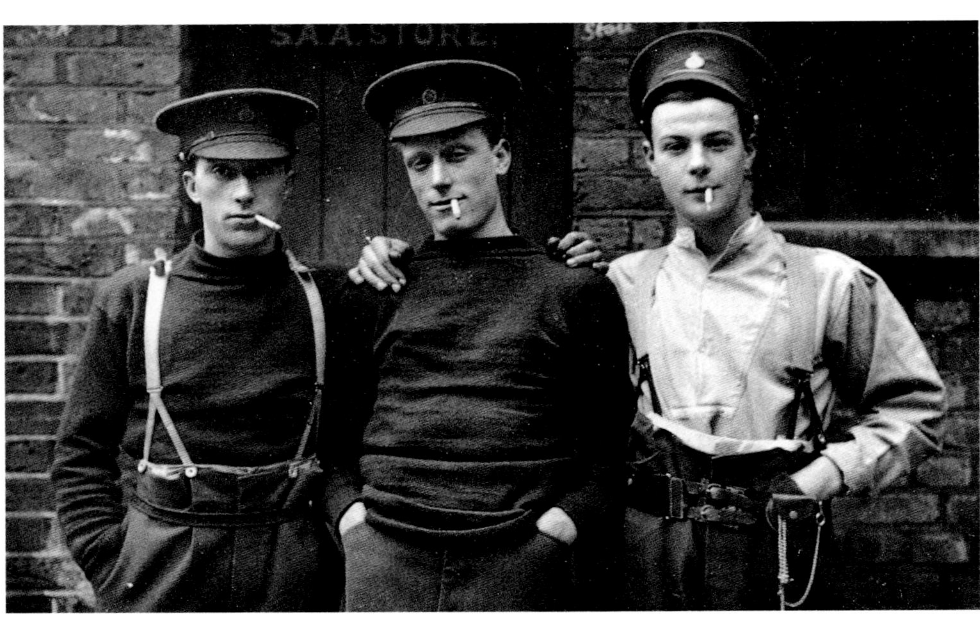

S.A.A. STORE.

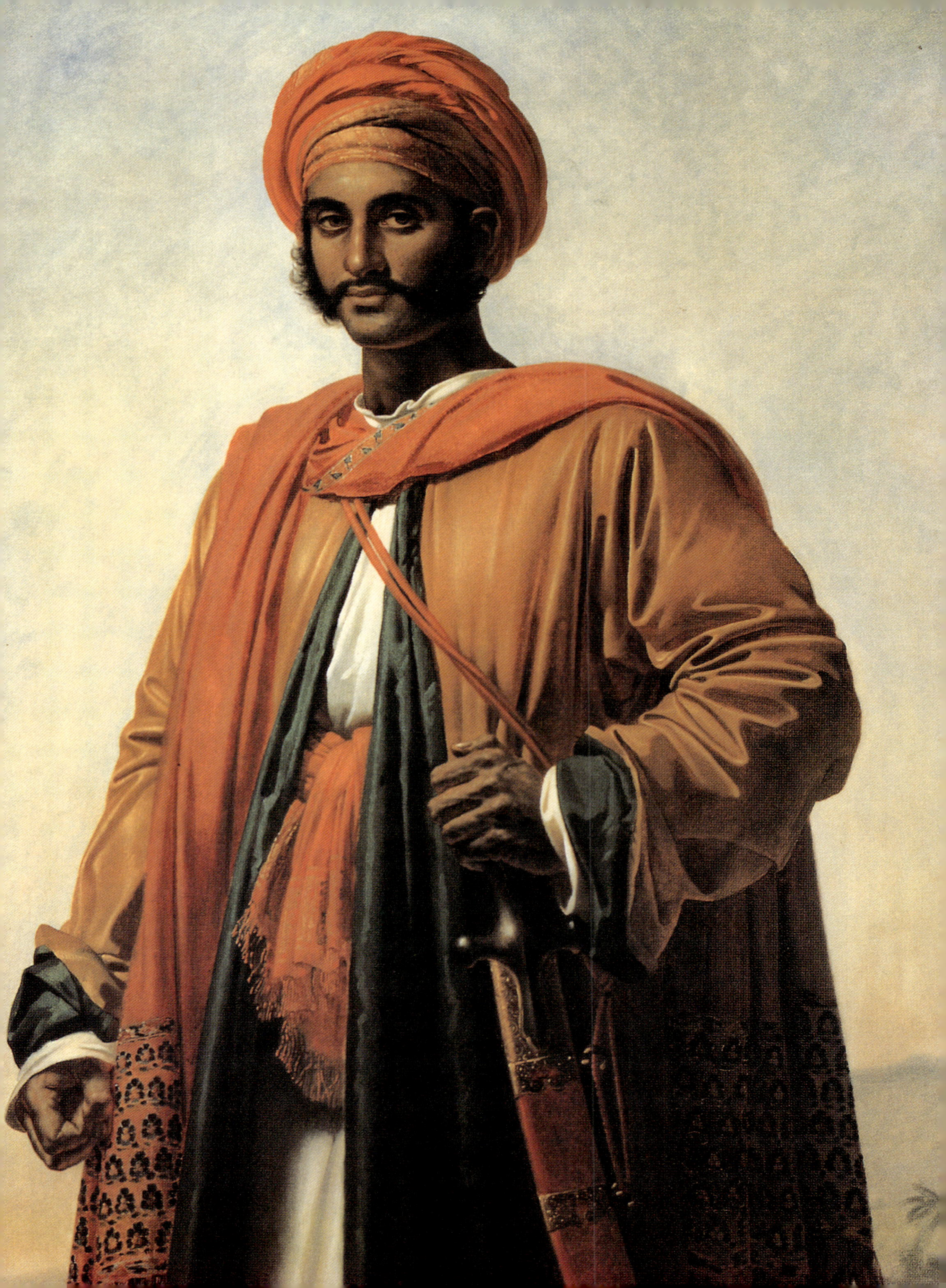

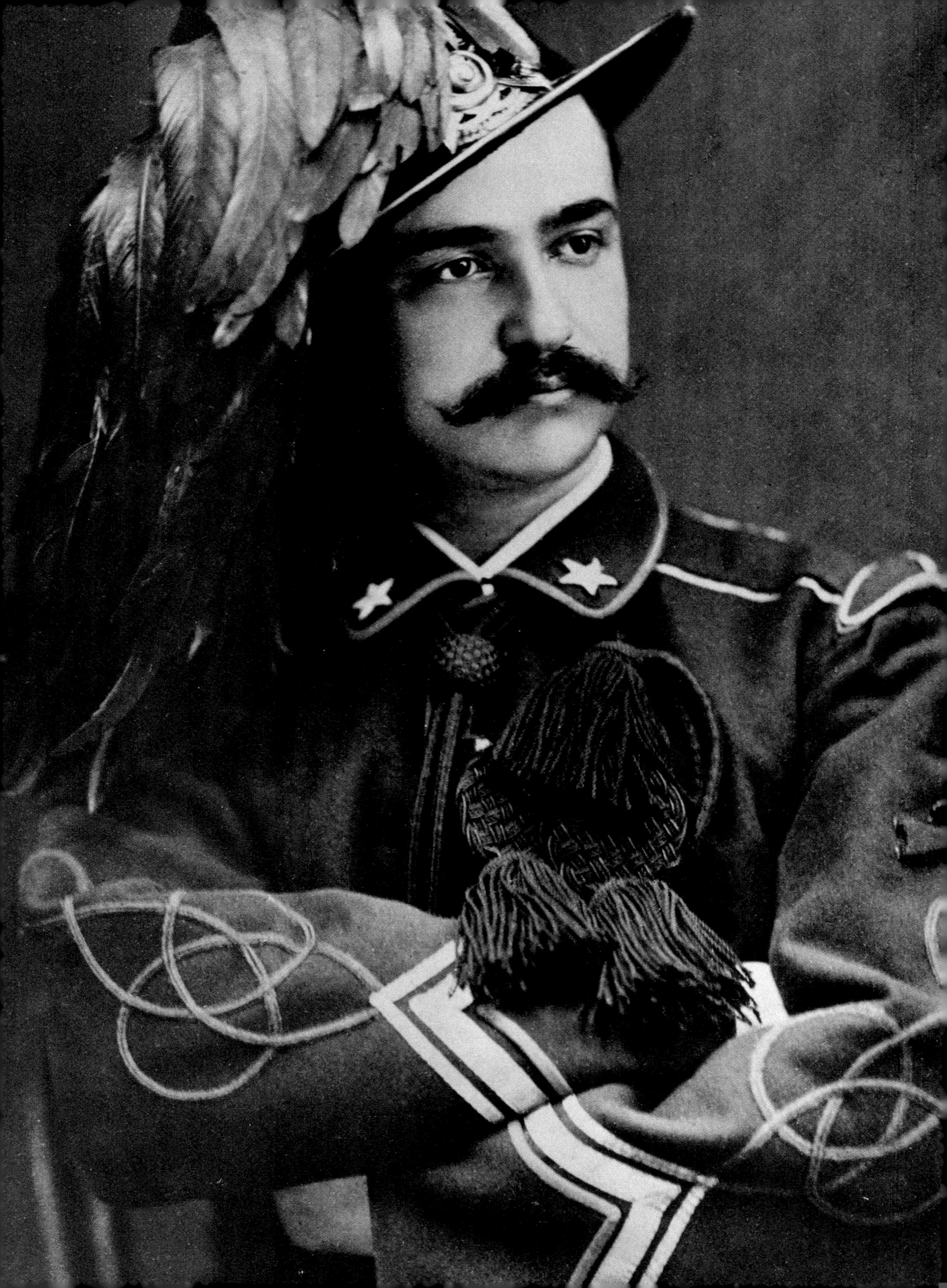

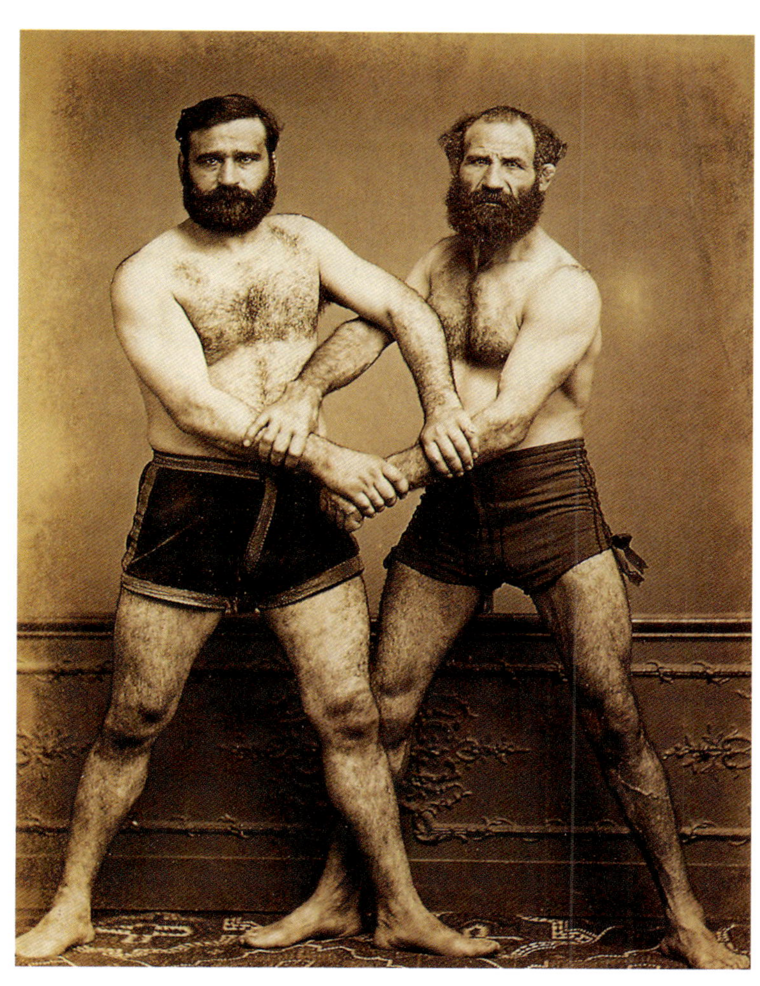

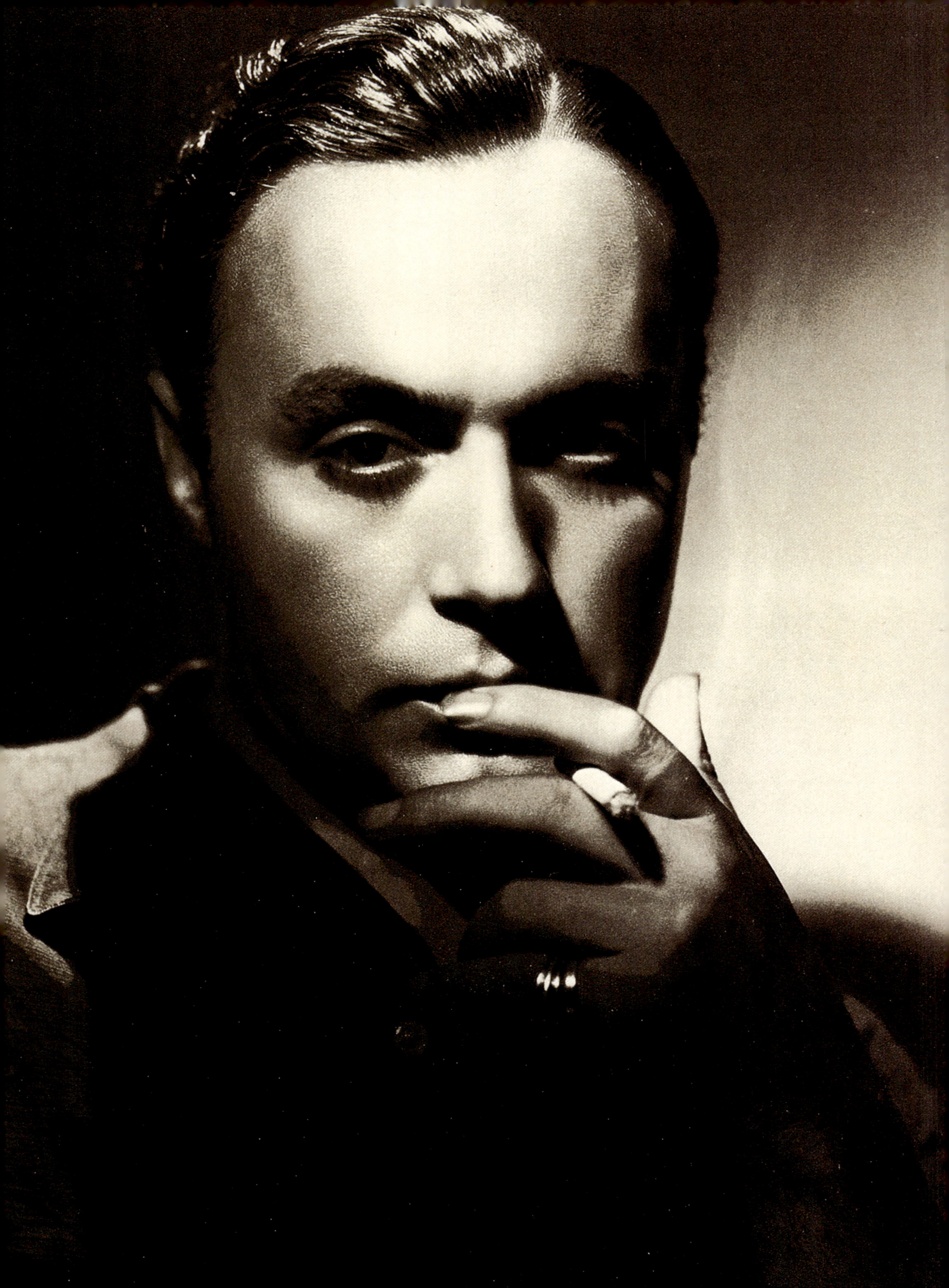

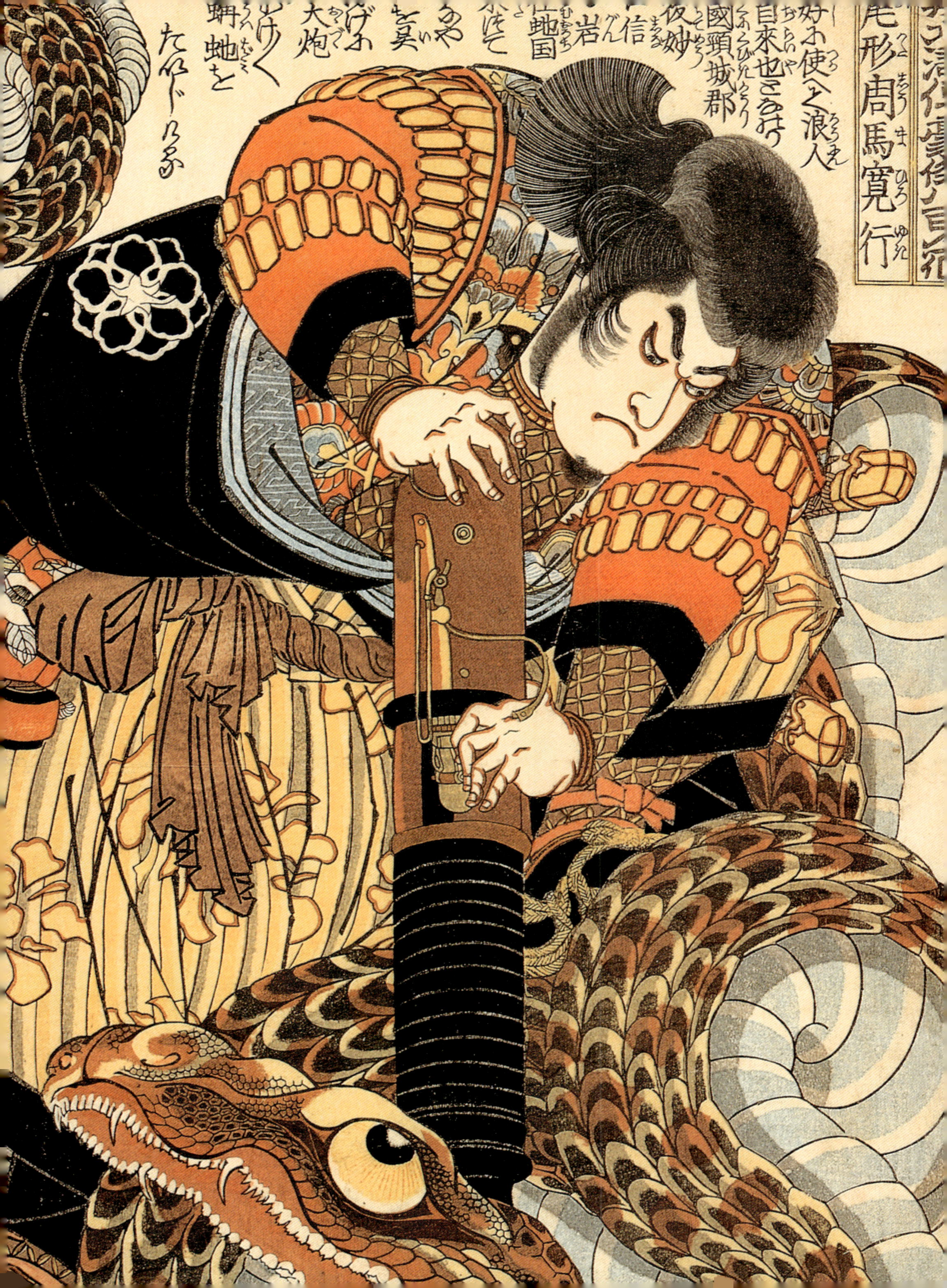

尾形周馬寛行
信濃国岩国頭城郡
国頭城郡
對ふ使へて浪人
目来也きのはや
夜妙
大炮
蝎蜒を
たけてみる

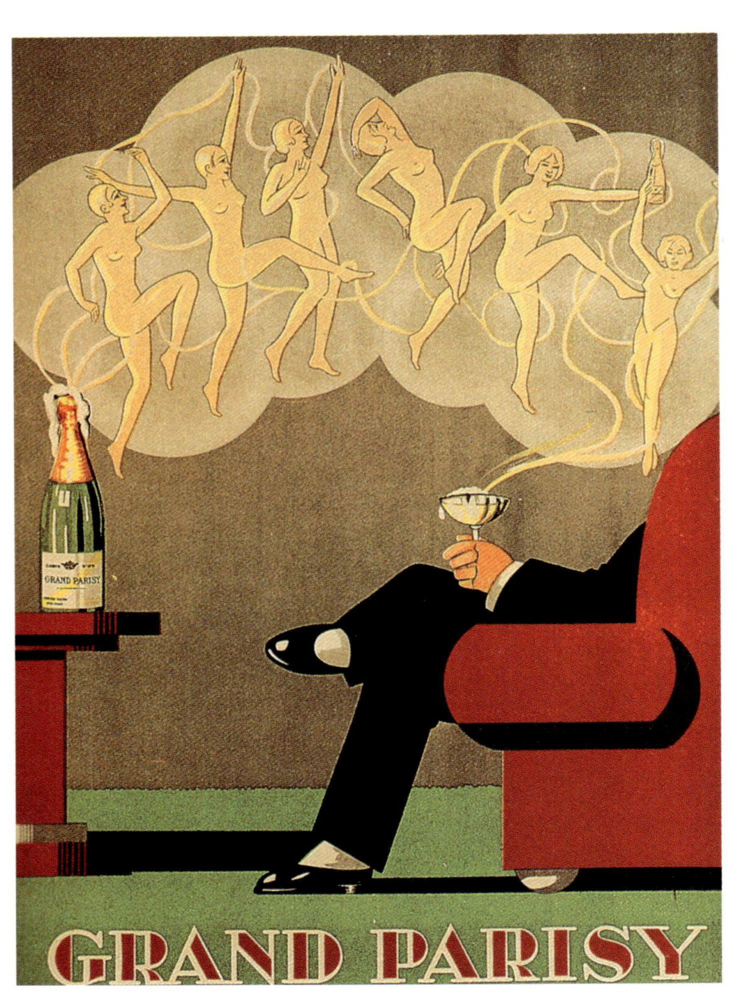
GRAND PARISY
GRAND PARISY

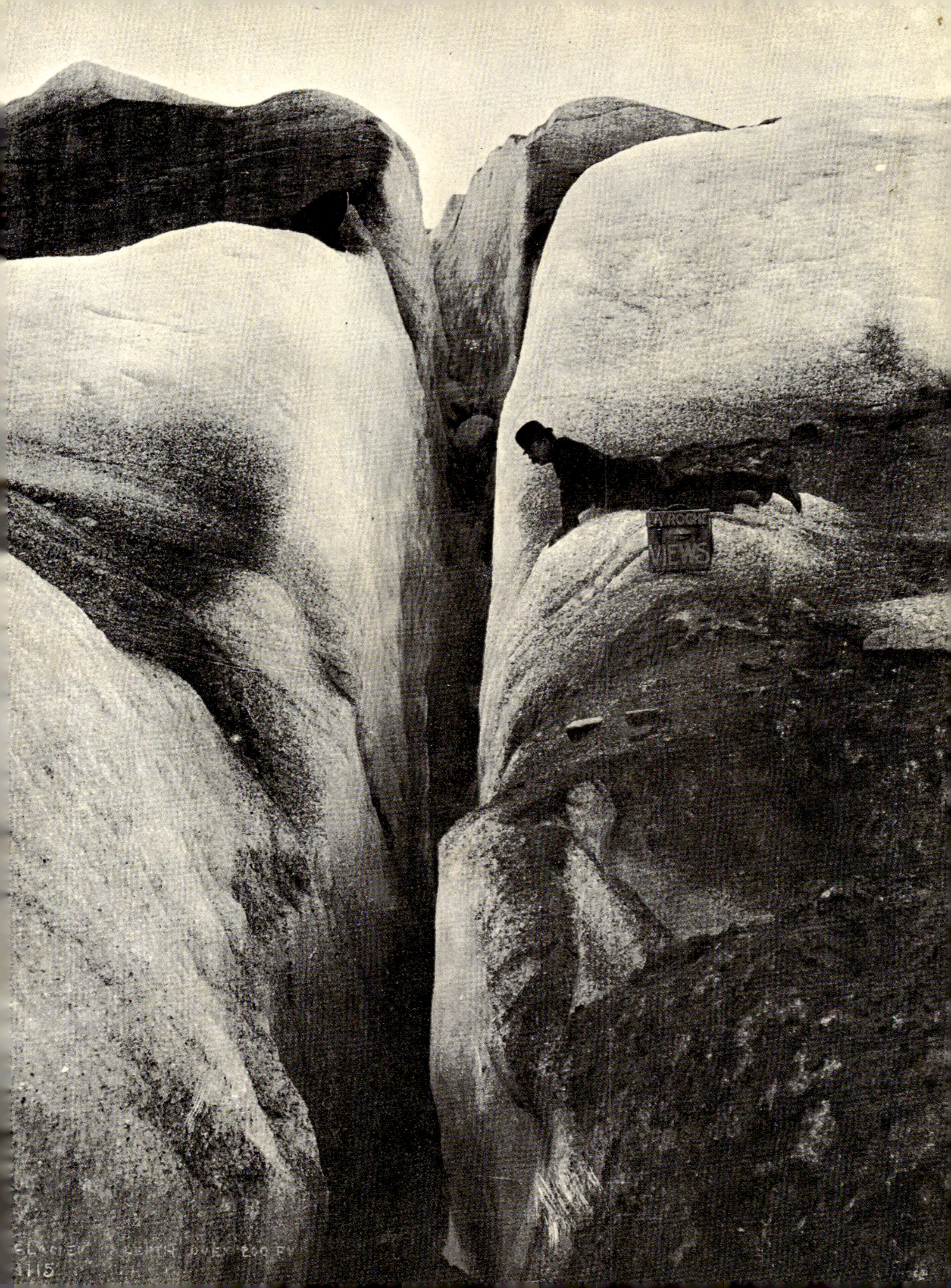

LA ROCHE
VIEWS
GLACIER DEPTH OVER 200 FT
1115

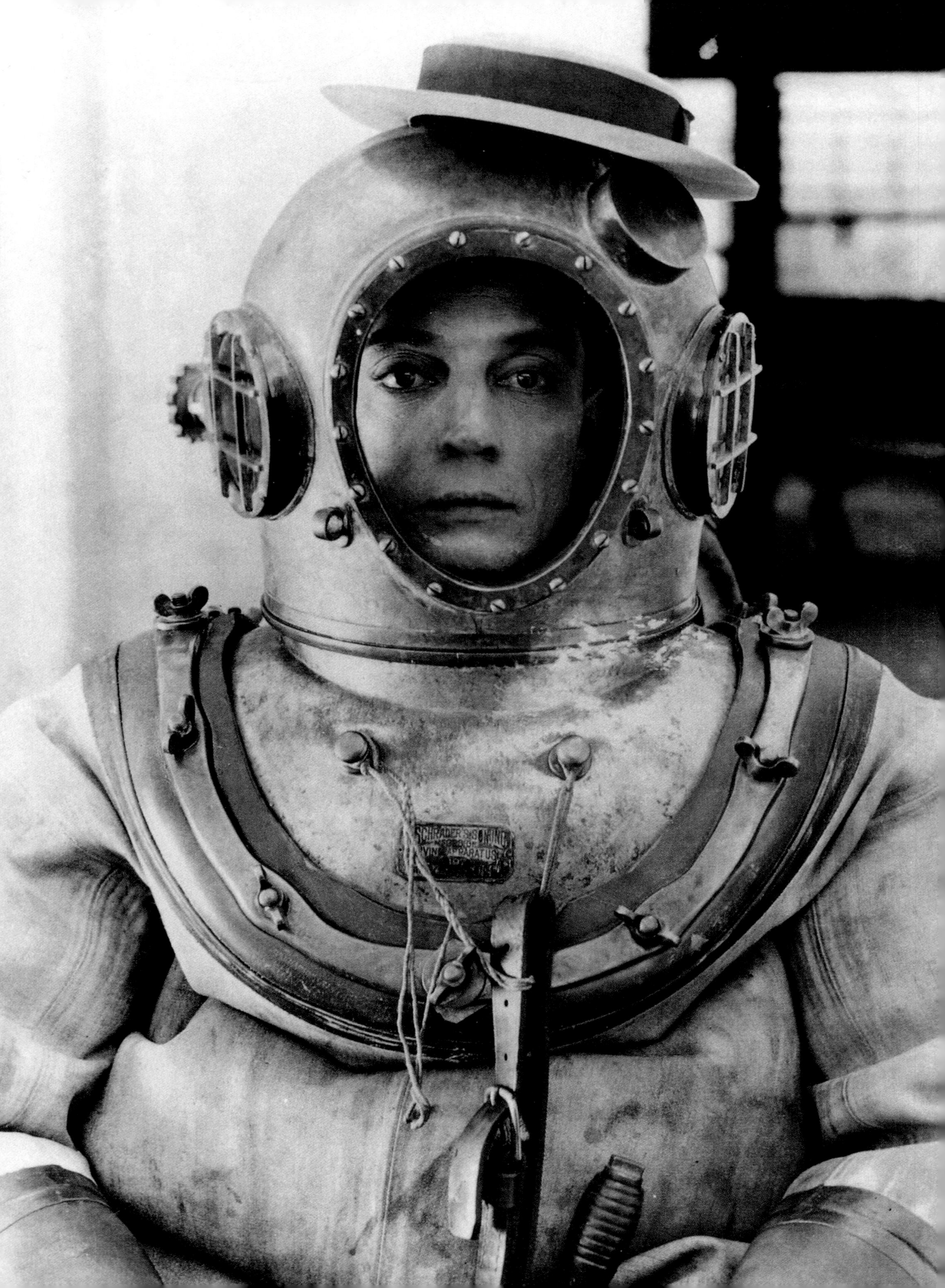

We are asleep with compasses in our hands.

W.S. Merwin

Do not believe the truth. The truth is tiny compared to what you have to do.

Leonard Cohen

How do I know what I think till I see what I say.

Wallace Stegner

When at any time there is a blundering or confusion in a maneuver, roll in amongst the soldiers and lay about you from right to left. This will convince people that it is not your fault.

Francis Grose: advice to officers, 1762

If I can't take what happens, I'm not ready for anything.

John Cage

To know the world one must construct it.

Cesare Pavese

"It's broccoli, dear."
"I say it's spinach, and I say the hell with it."

E.B. White

We keep our distance. It is all we have.

Richard Shelton

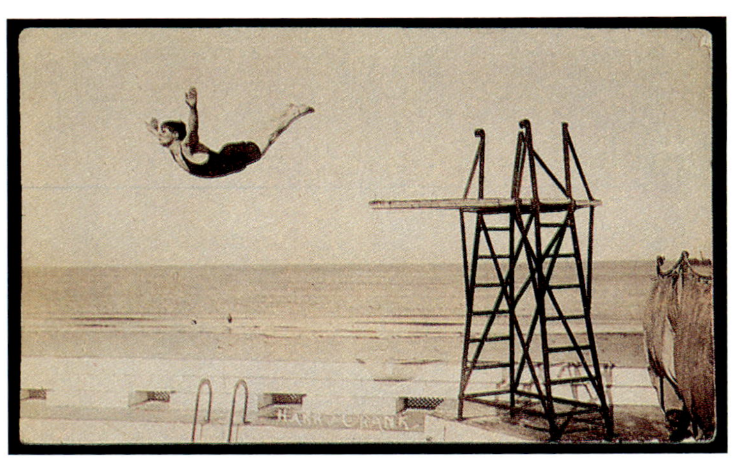

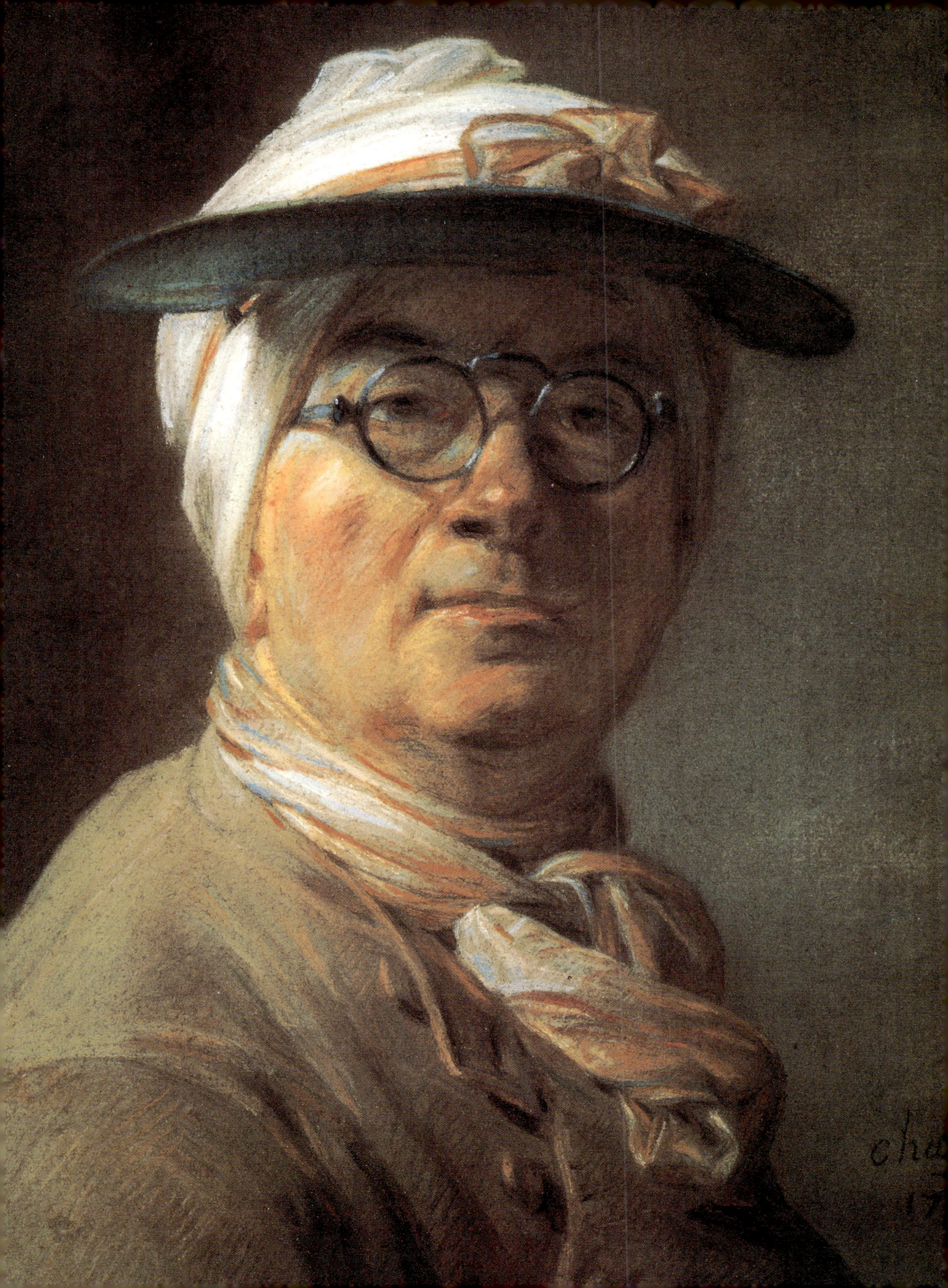
cha

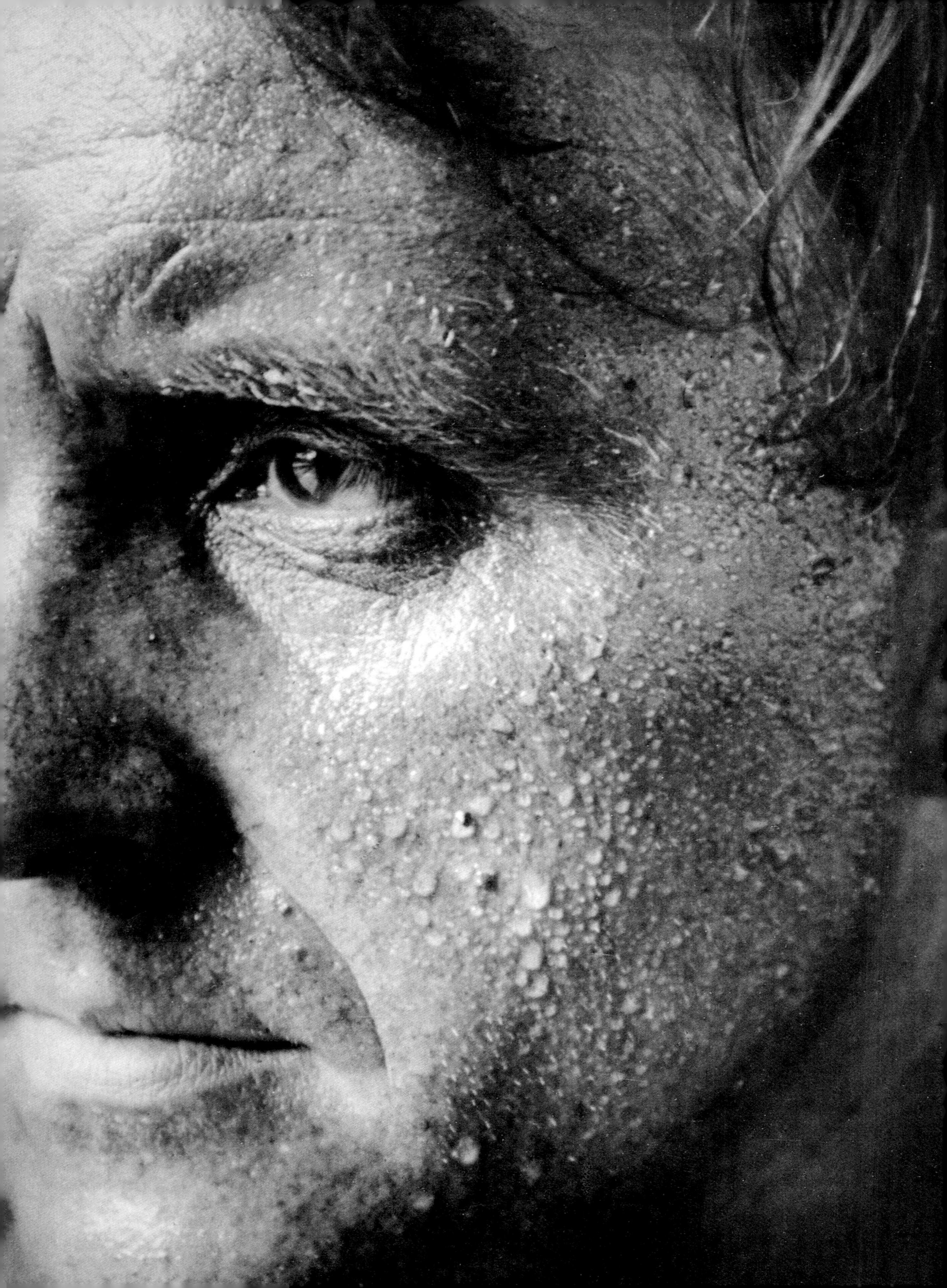

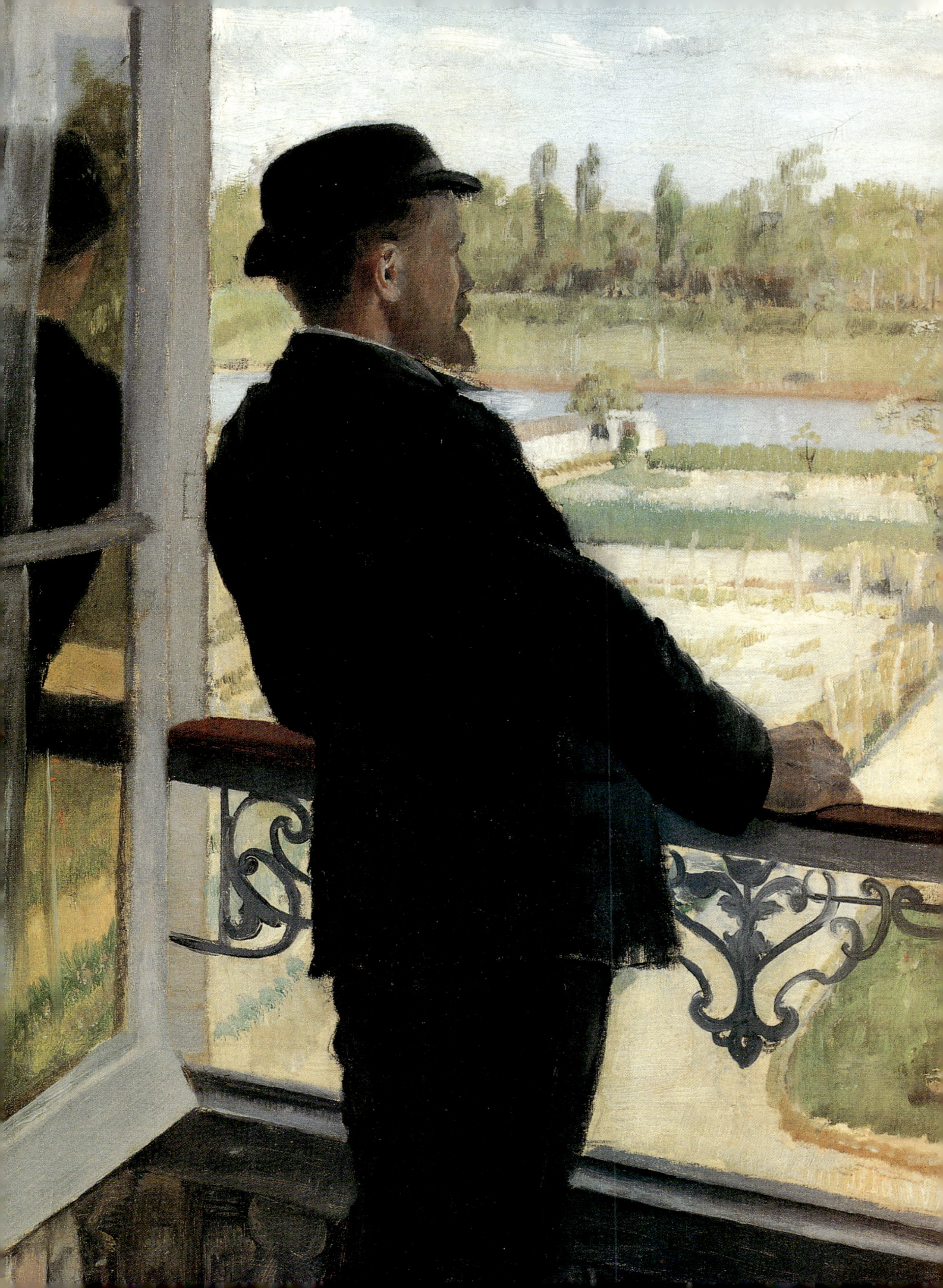

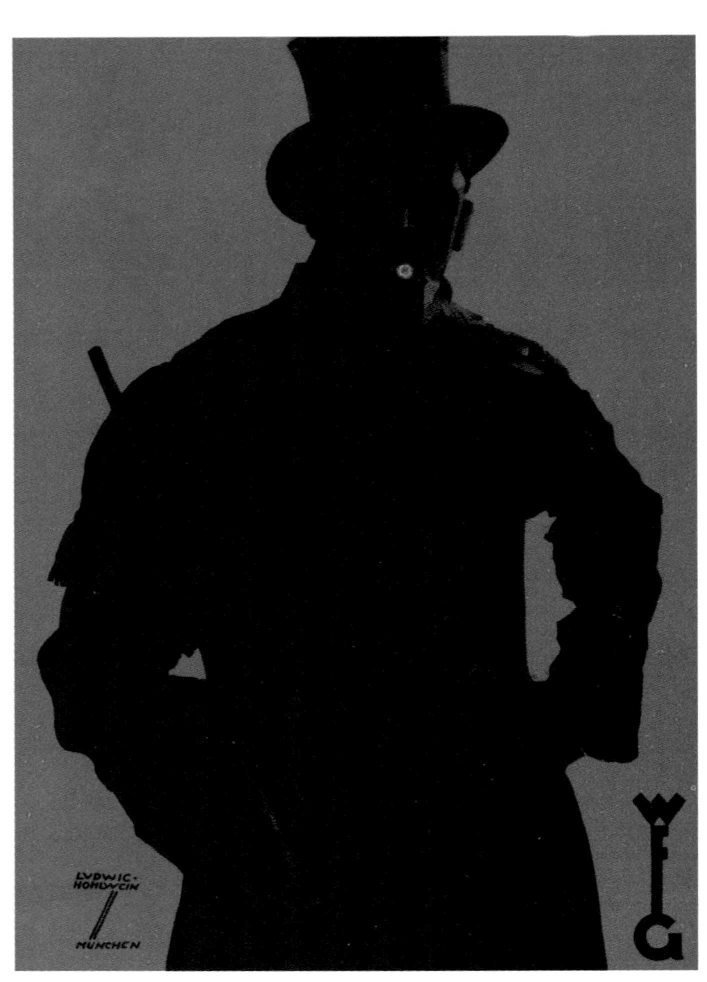

LVDWIG·
HOHLWEIN
MÜNCHEN
WFG

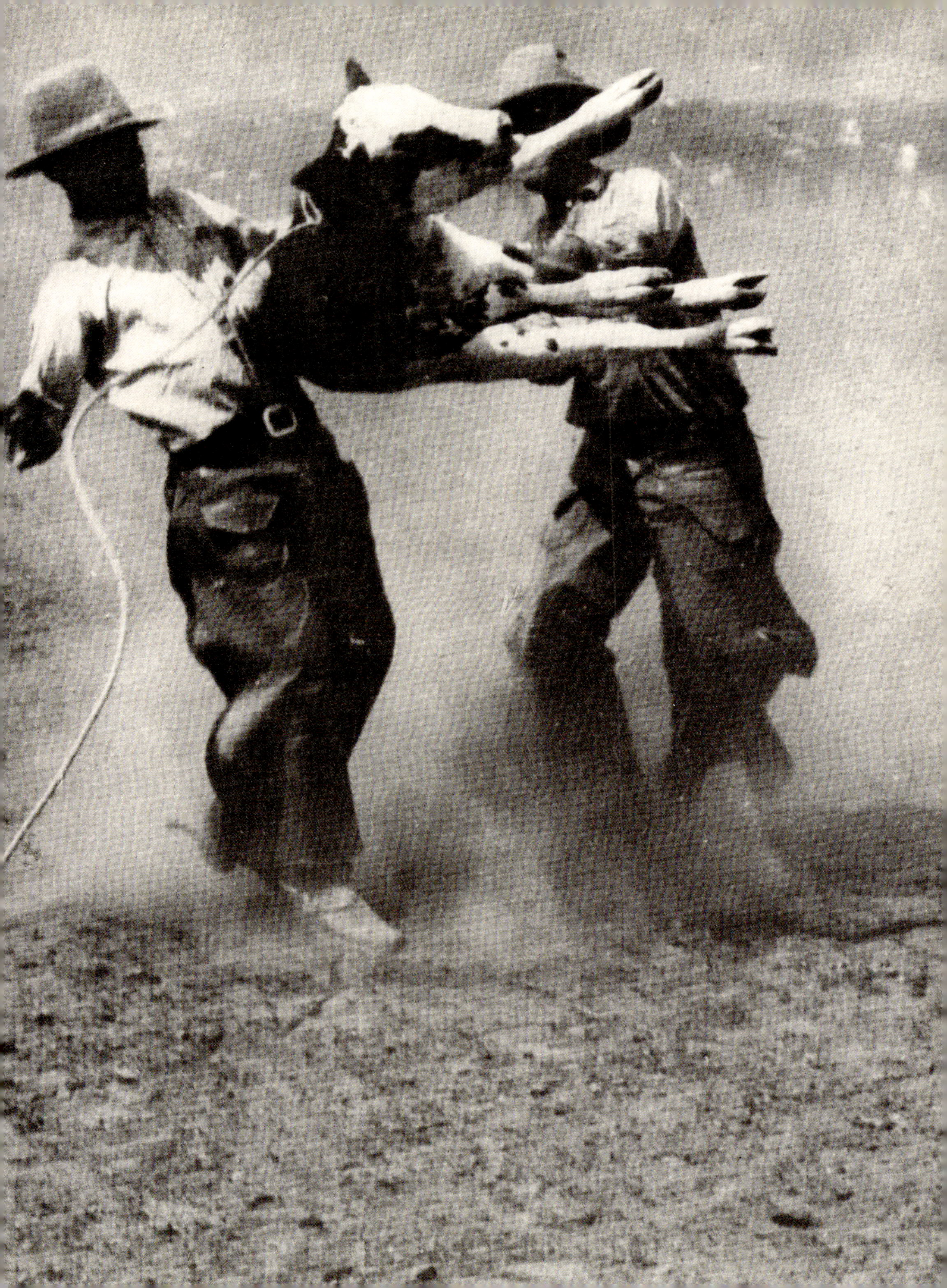

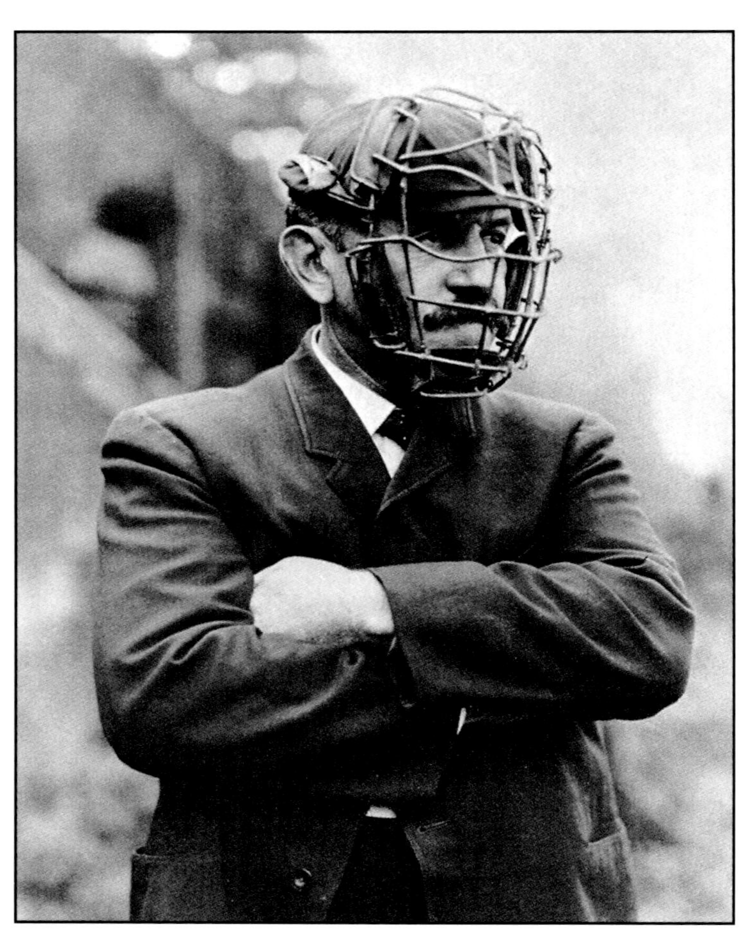

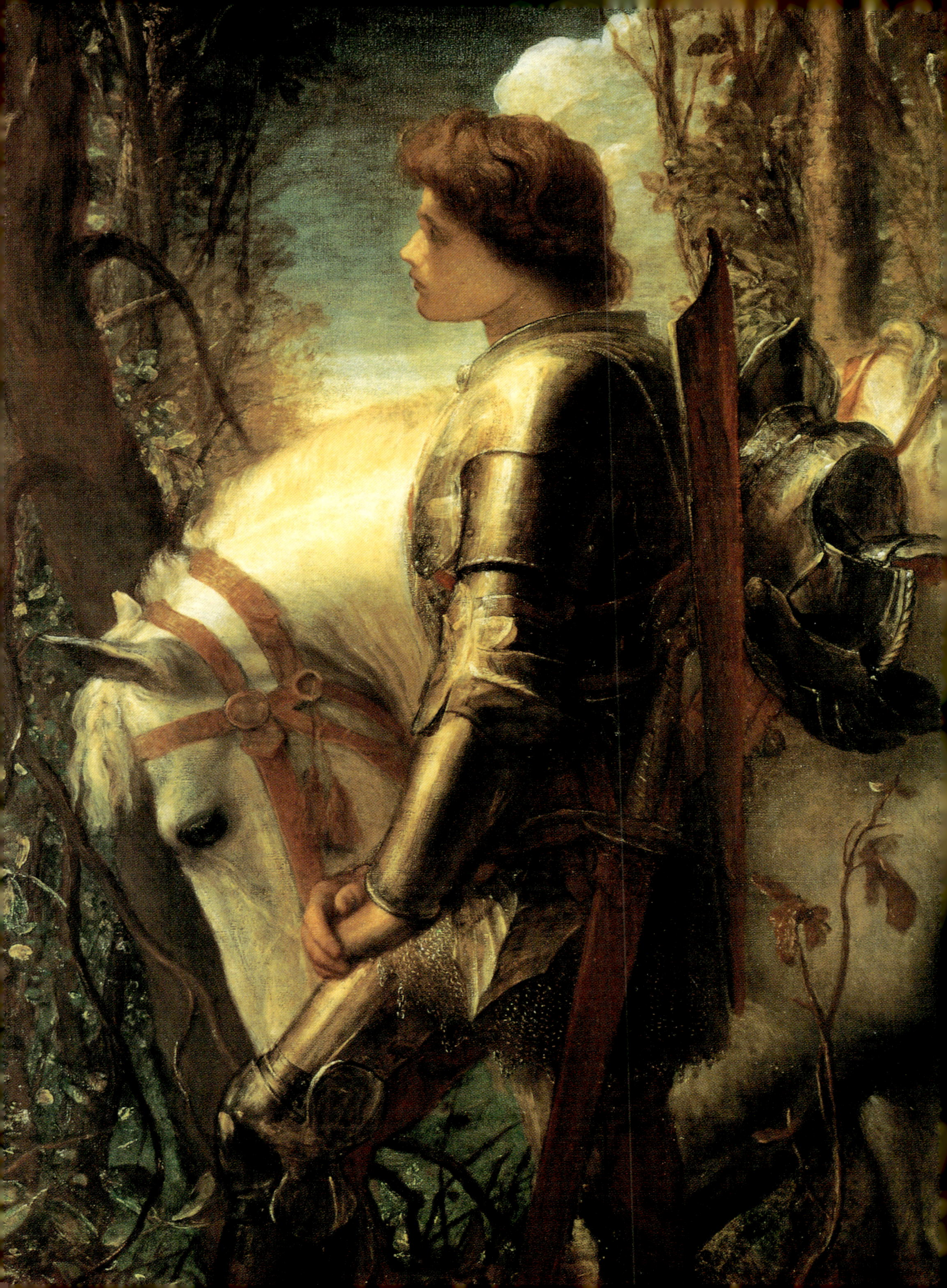

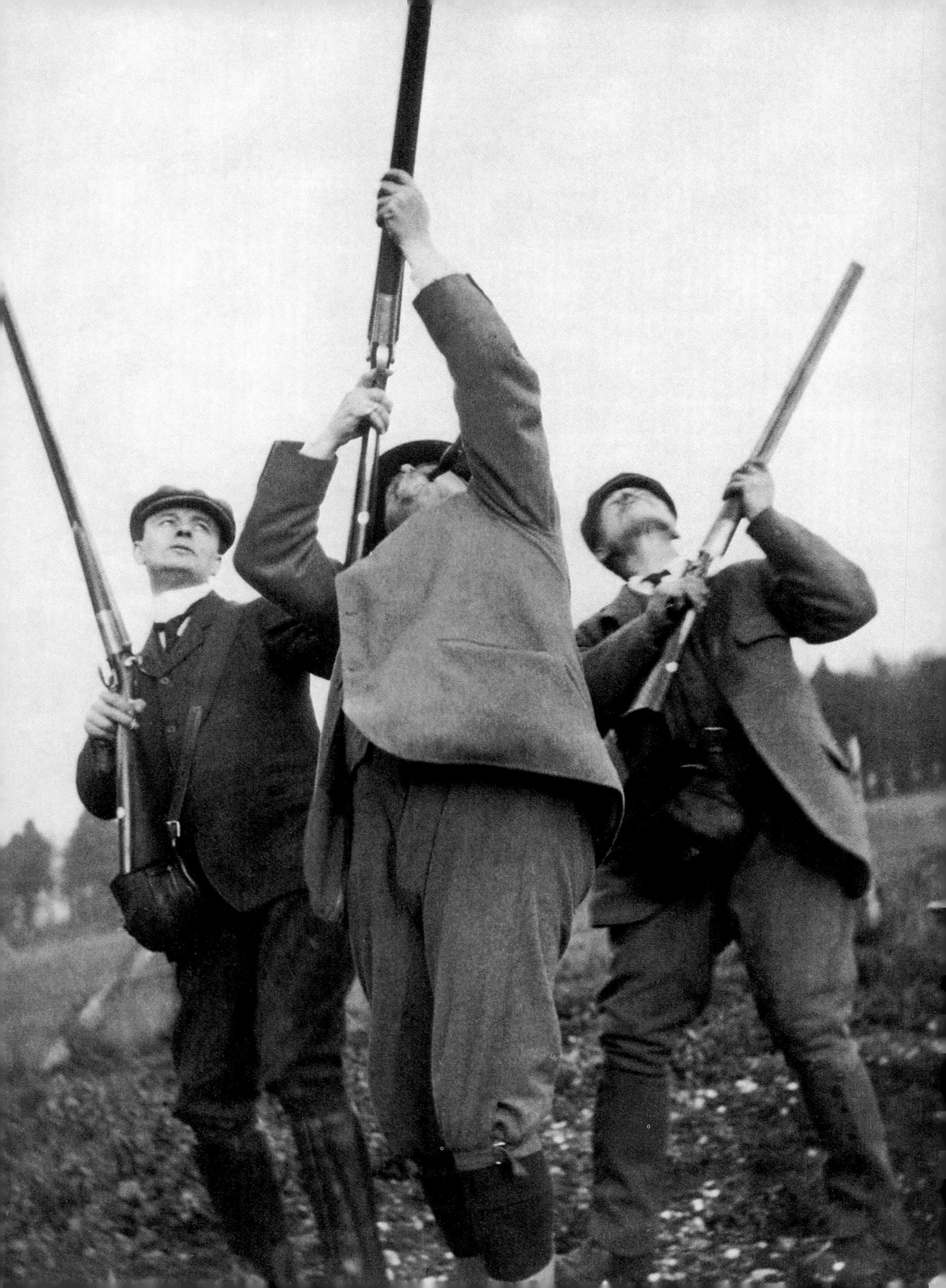

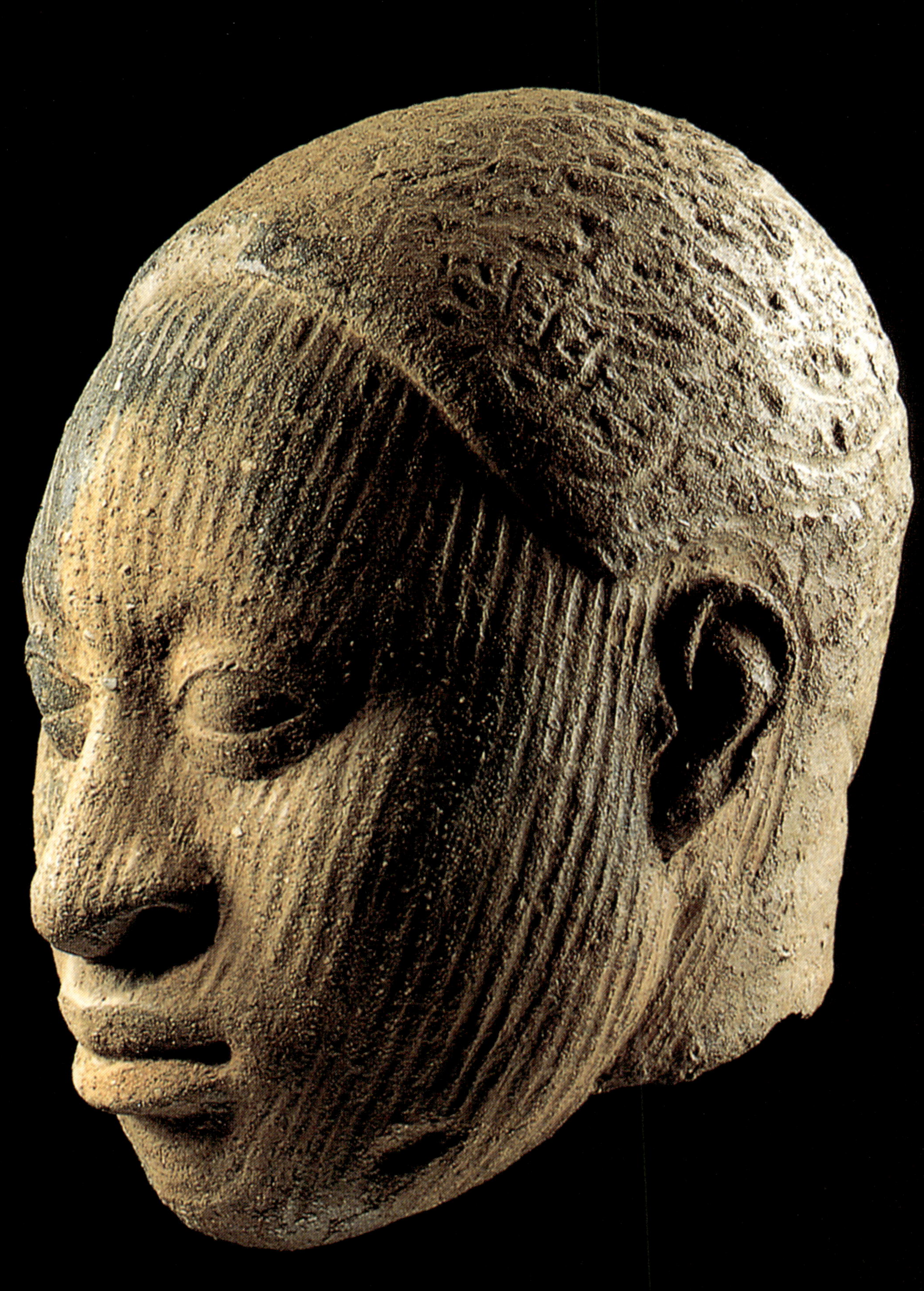

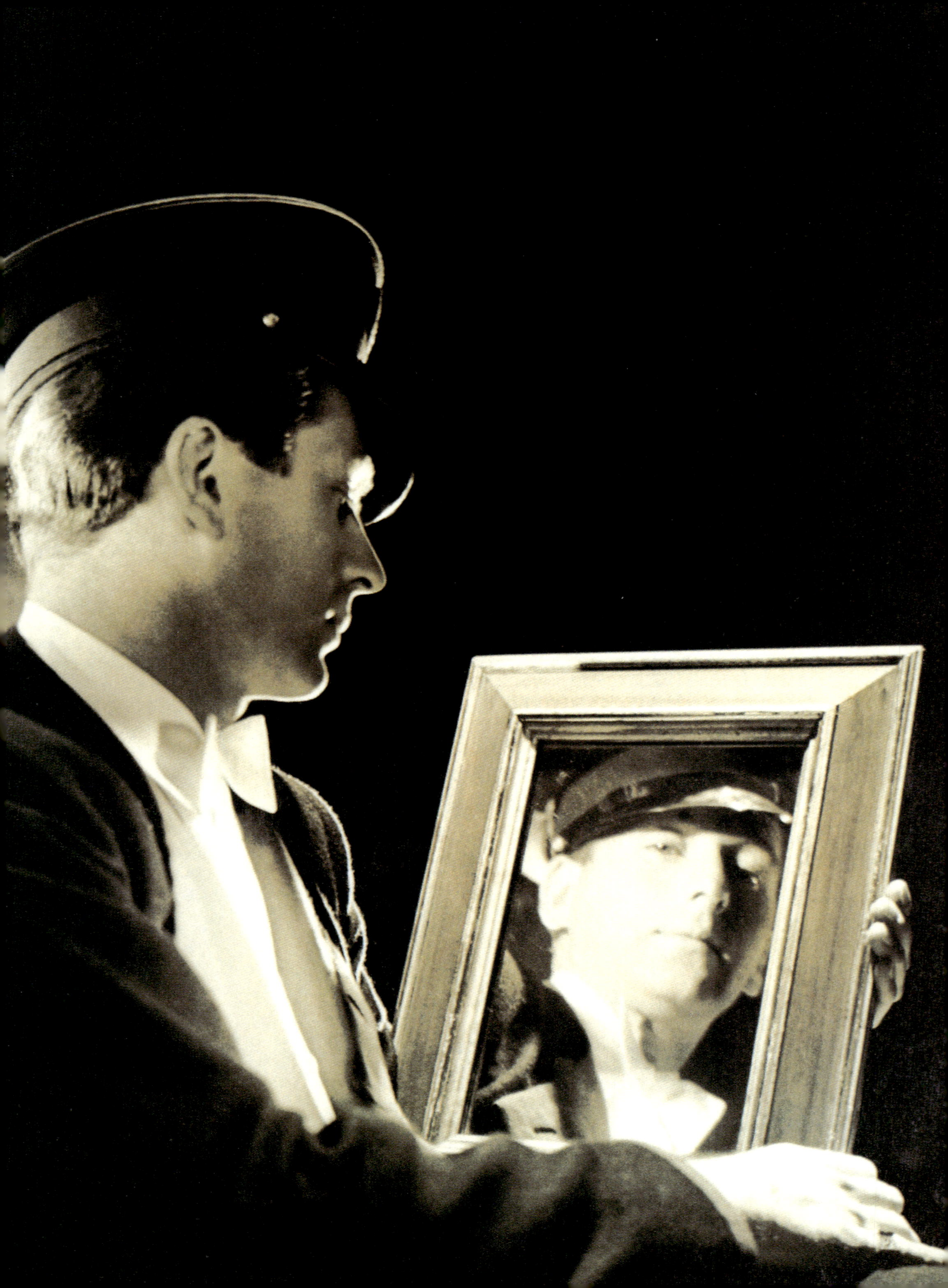

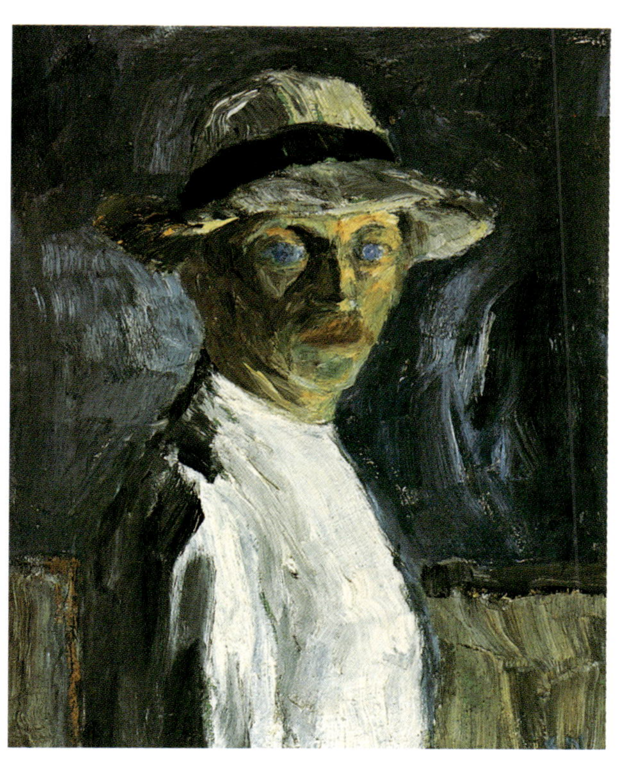

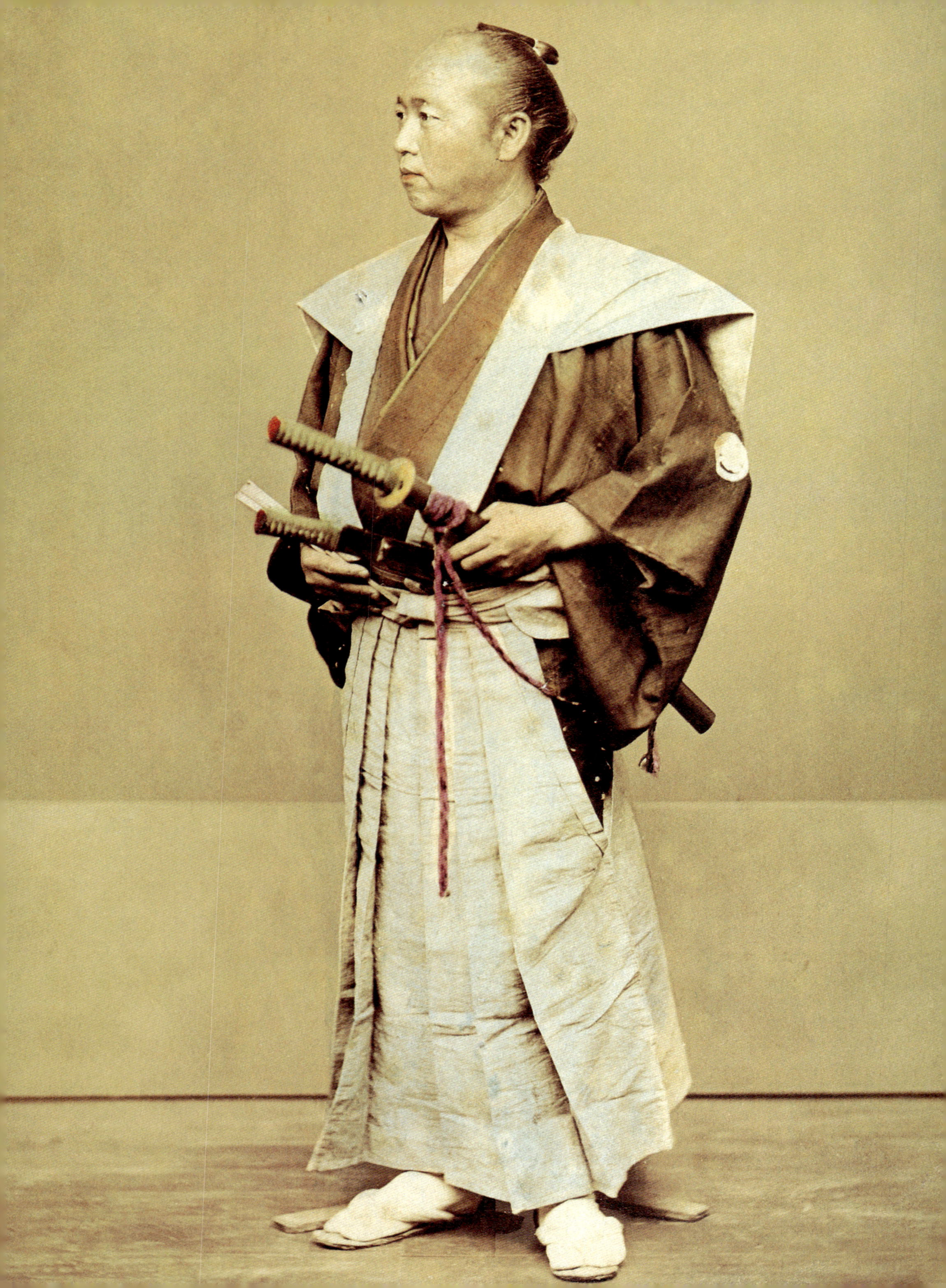

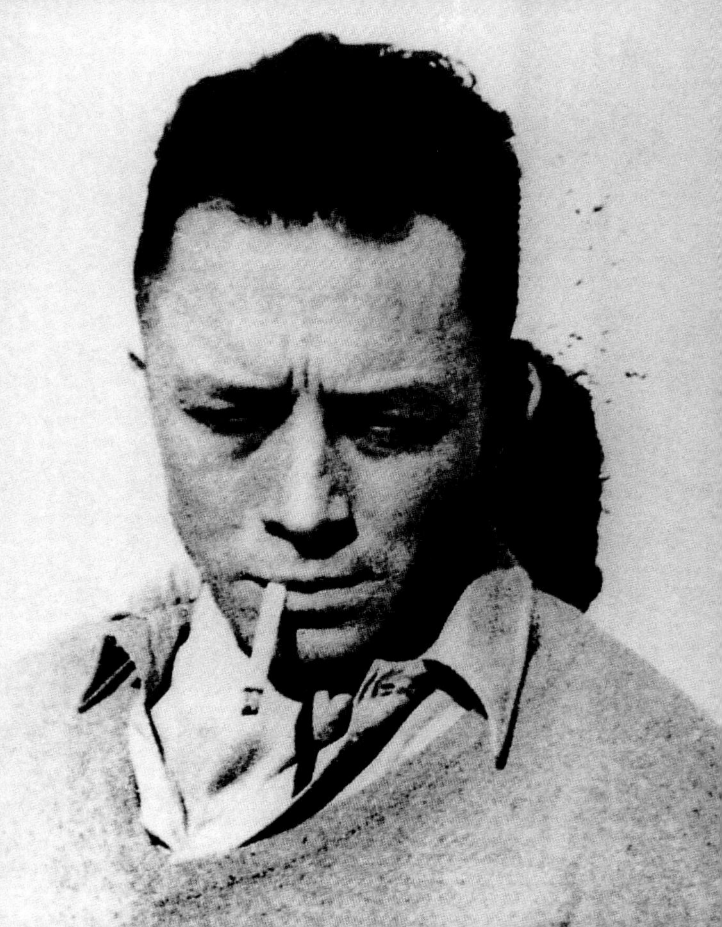

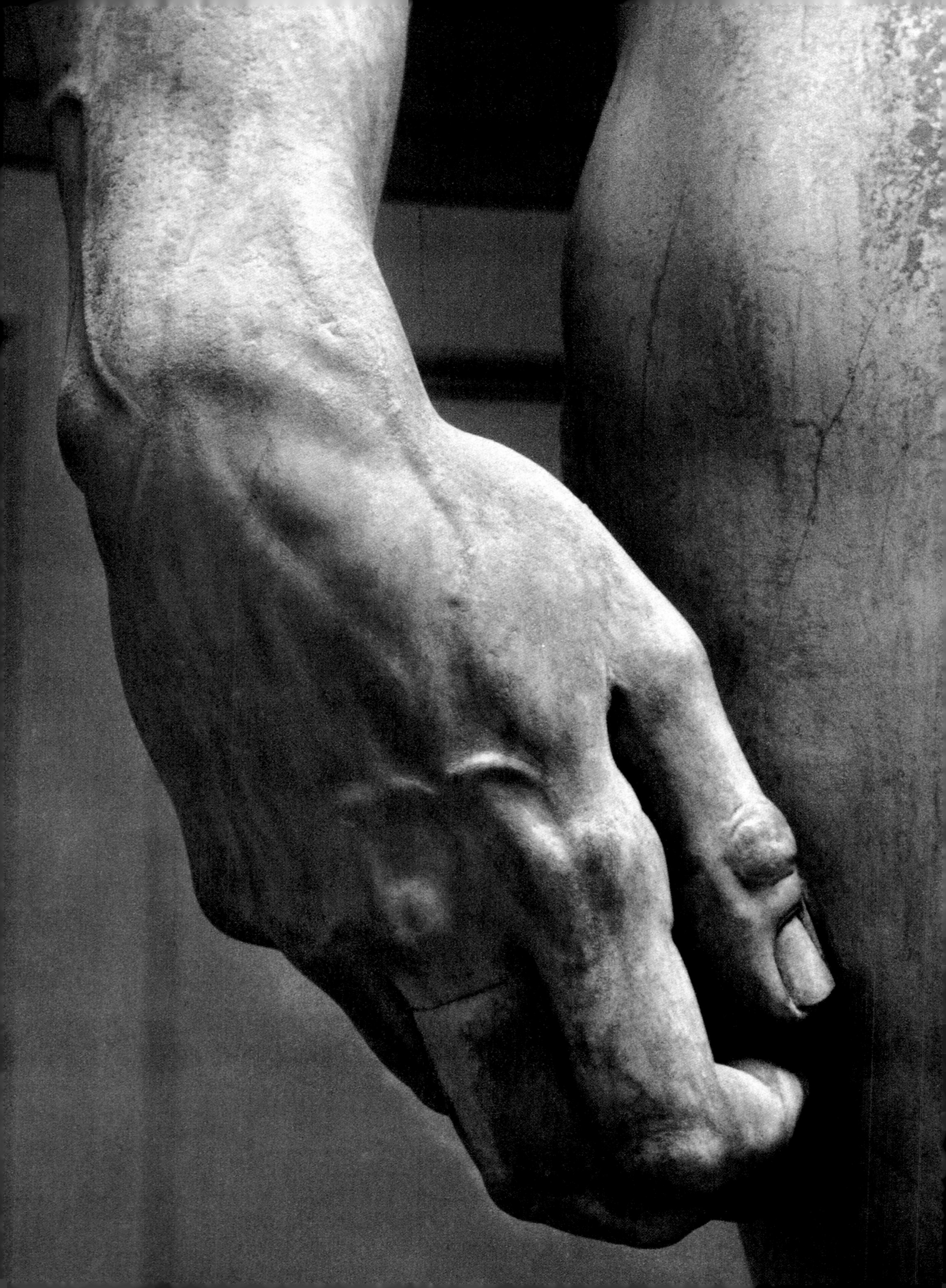

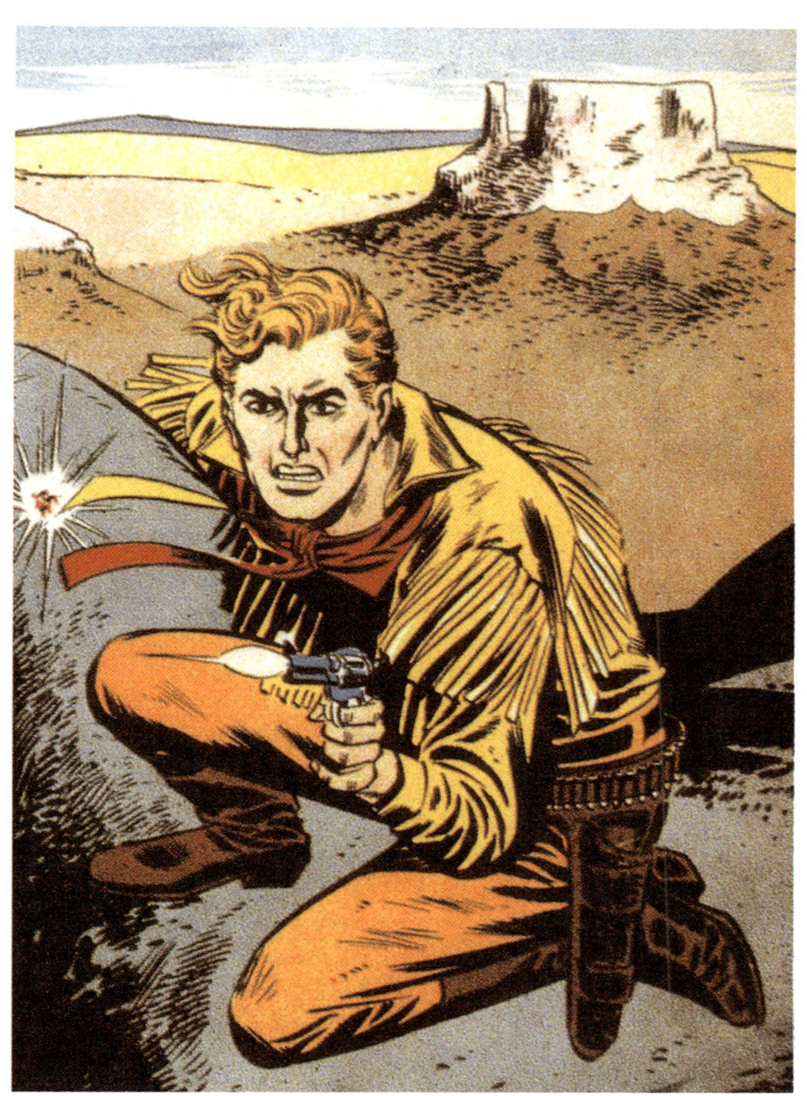

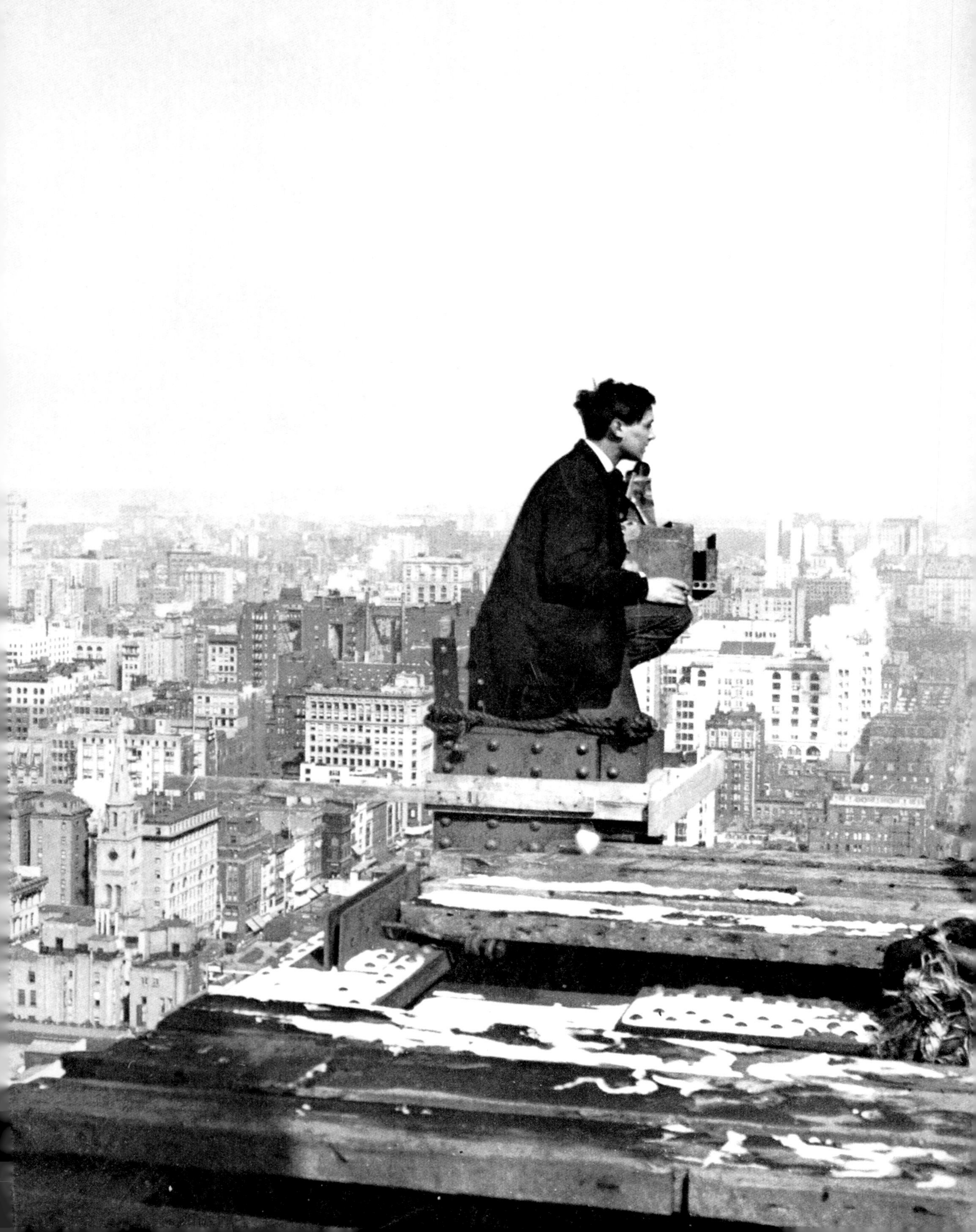

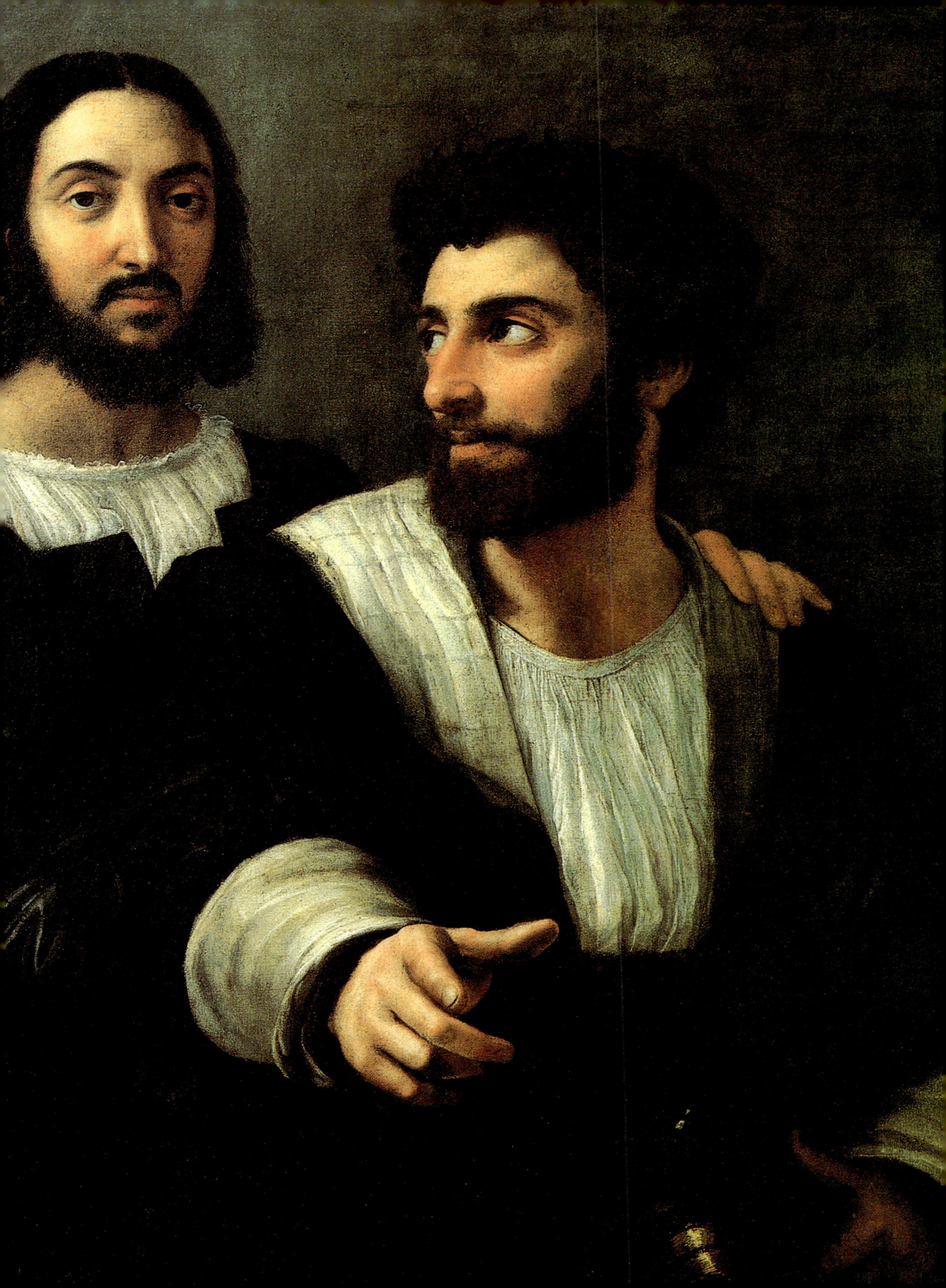

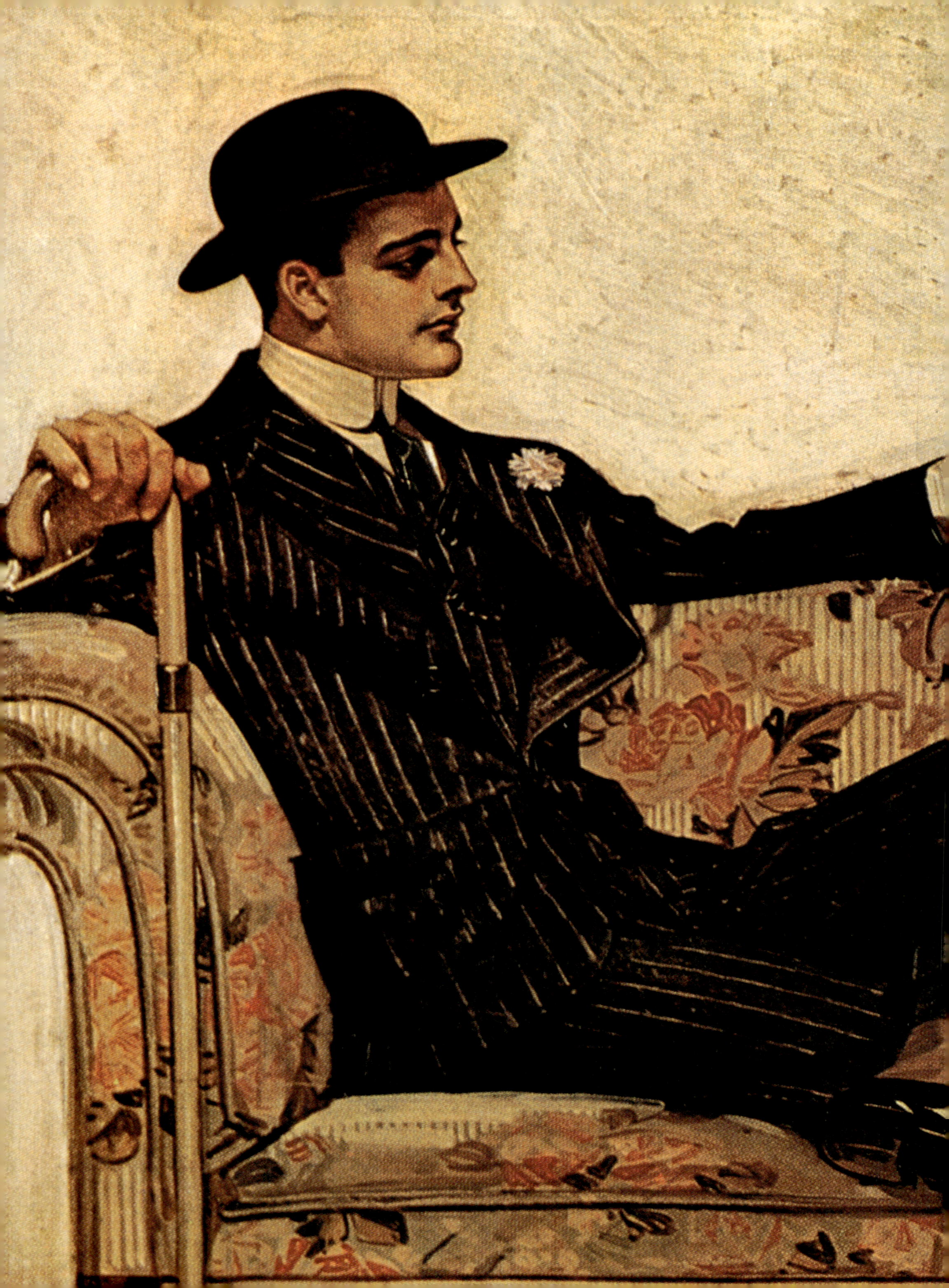

I am the least difficult of men.  All I want is boundless love.

Frank O'Hara

I must have a prodigious quality of mind; it takes me as much as a week sometimes to make it up.

Mark Twain

… a good billiard table, a rowing boat, a wife, or some other dream of bliss.

Gustave Flaubert

Creativity in science could be described as the act of putting two and two together to make five.

Arthur Koestler

It is easy to image a language consisting only of questions and expressions for answering yes and no.

Ludwig Wittgenstein

Speer survived in prison partly by persisting in a series of elaborate games, creations that he describes as "the organization of emptiness."  He converted his walks around the prison yard into a walk around the world, studying guidebooks and charting on a map his progress across Afghanistan, up the coast of China. One day, while promenading with Hess, Speer startled his companion by suddenly announcing that they were only an hour from the Bering Strait.

Unknown

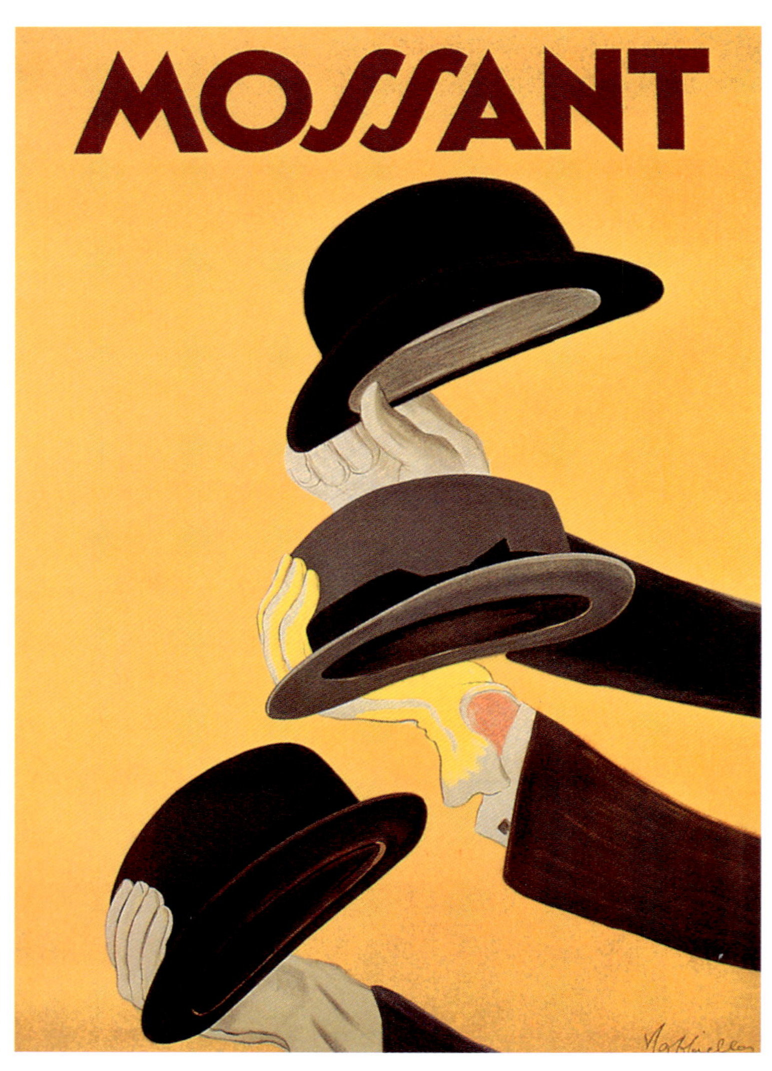

MOSSANT

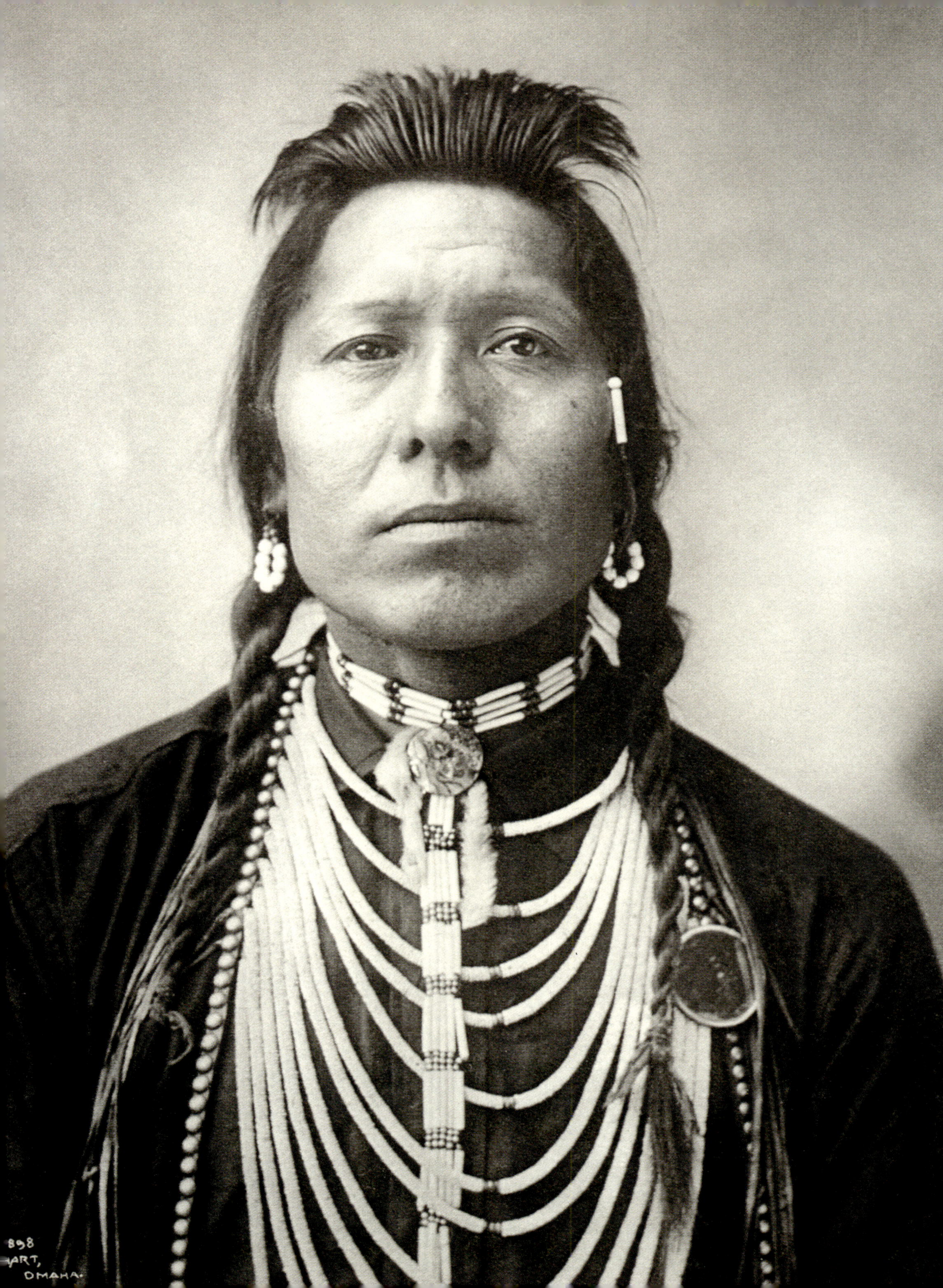
898
ART,
OMAHA.

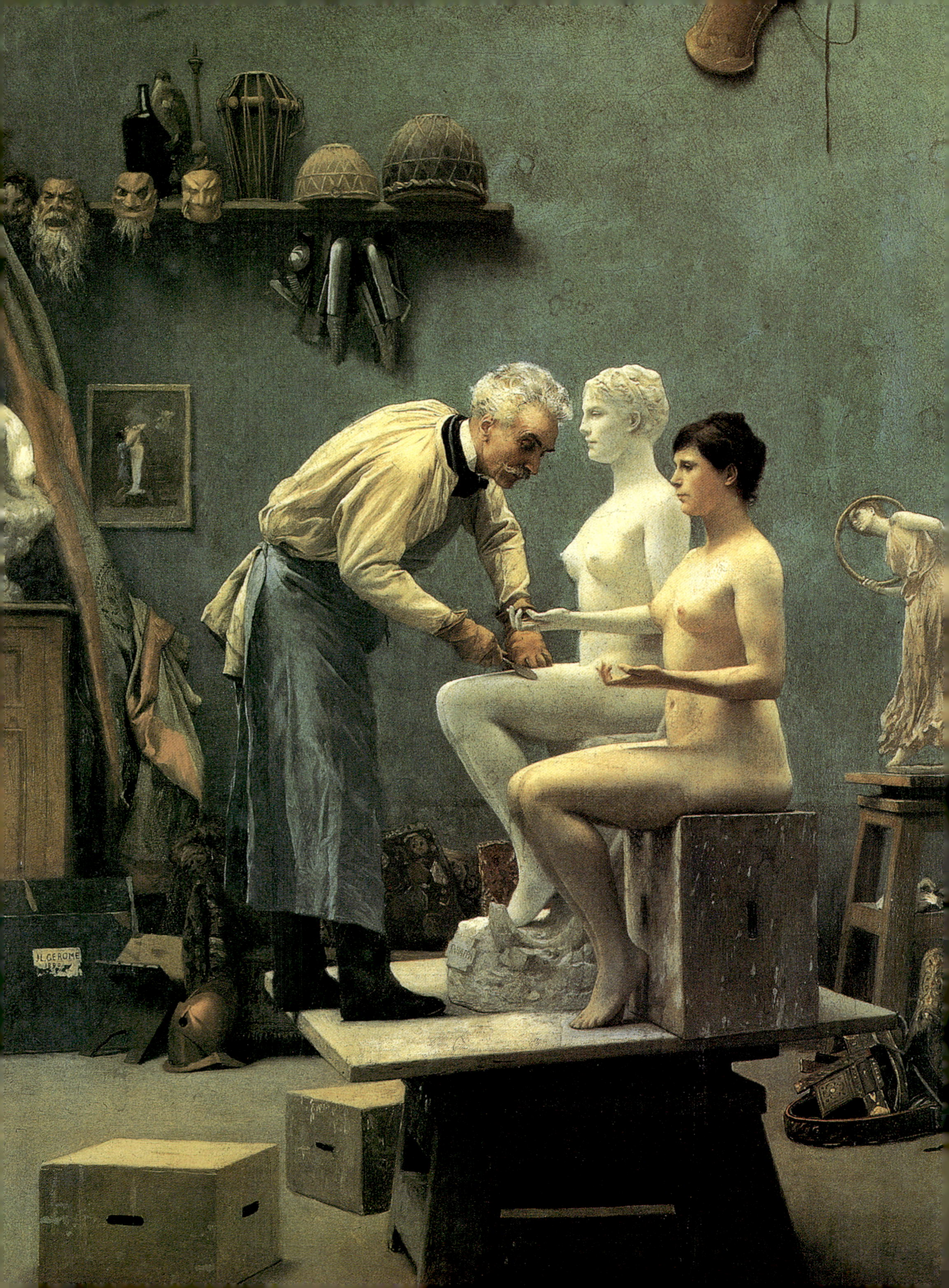
JL. GÉROME
1890

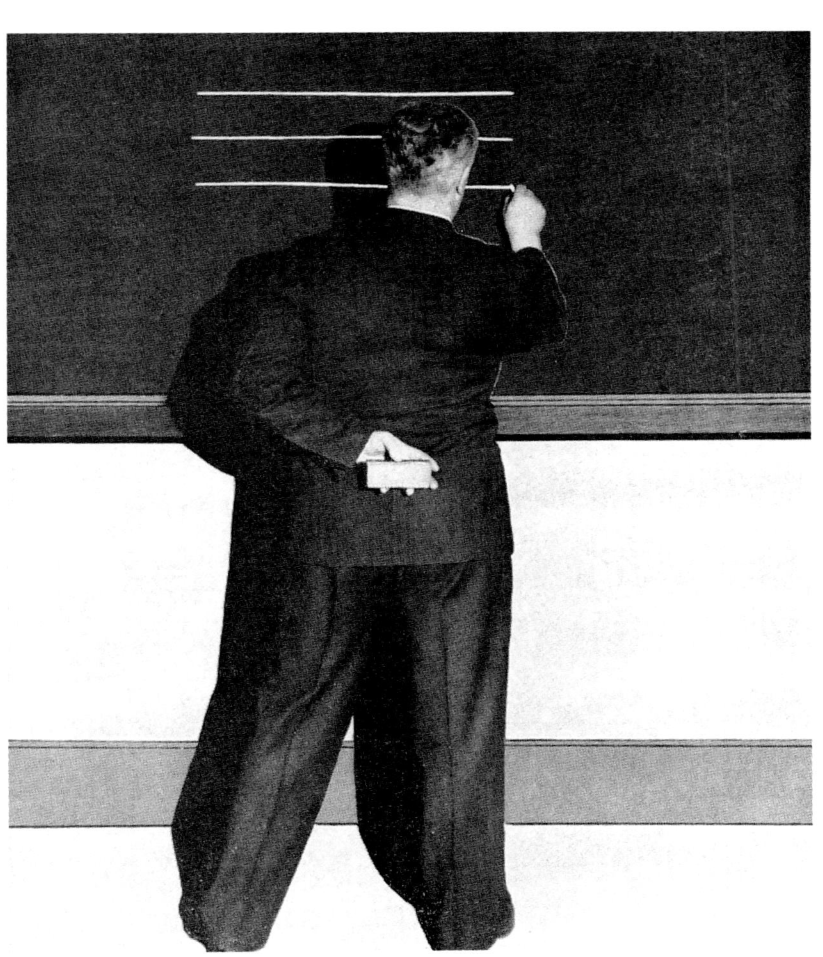

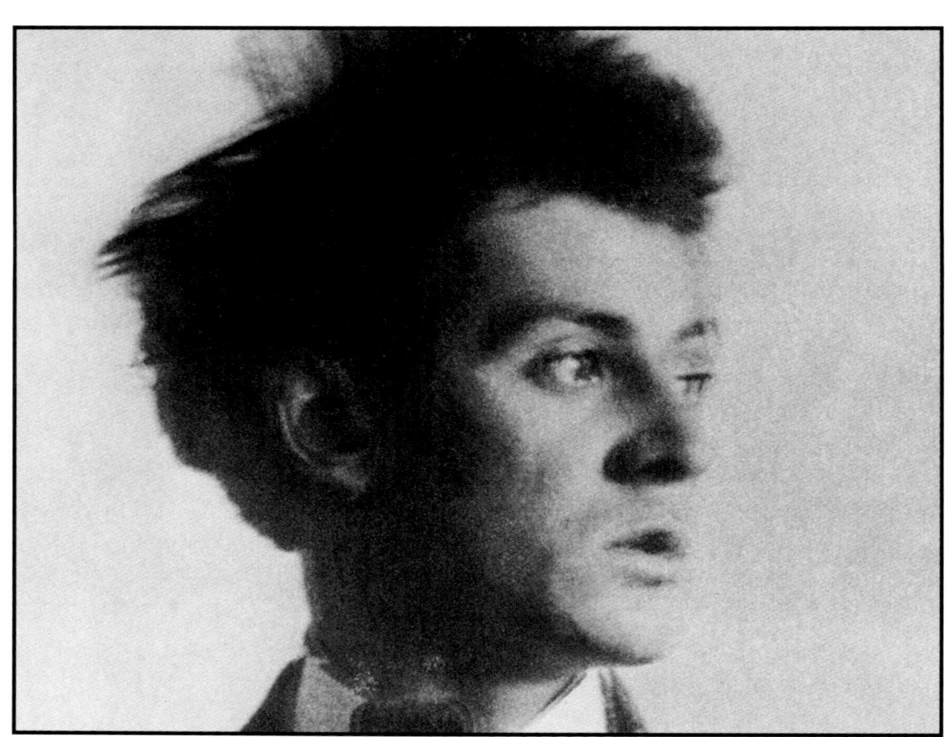

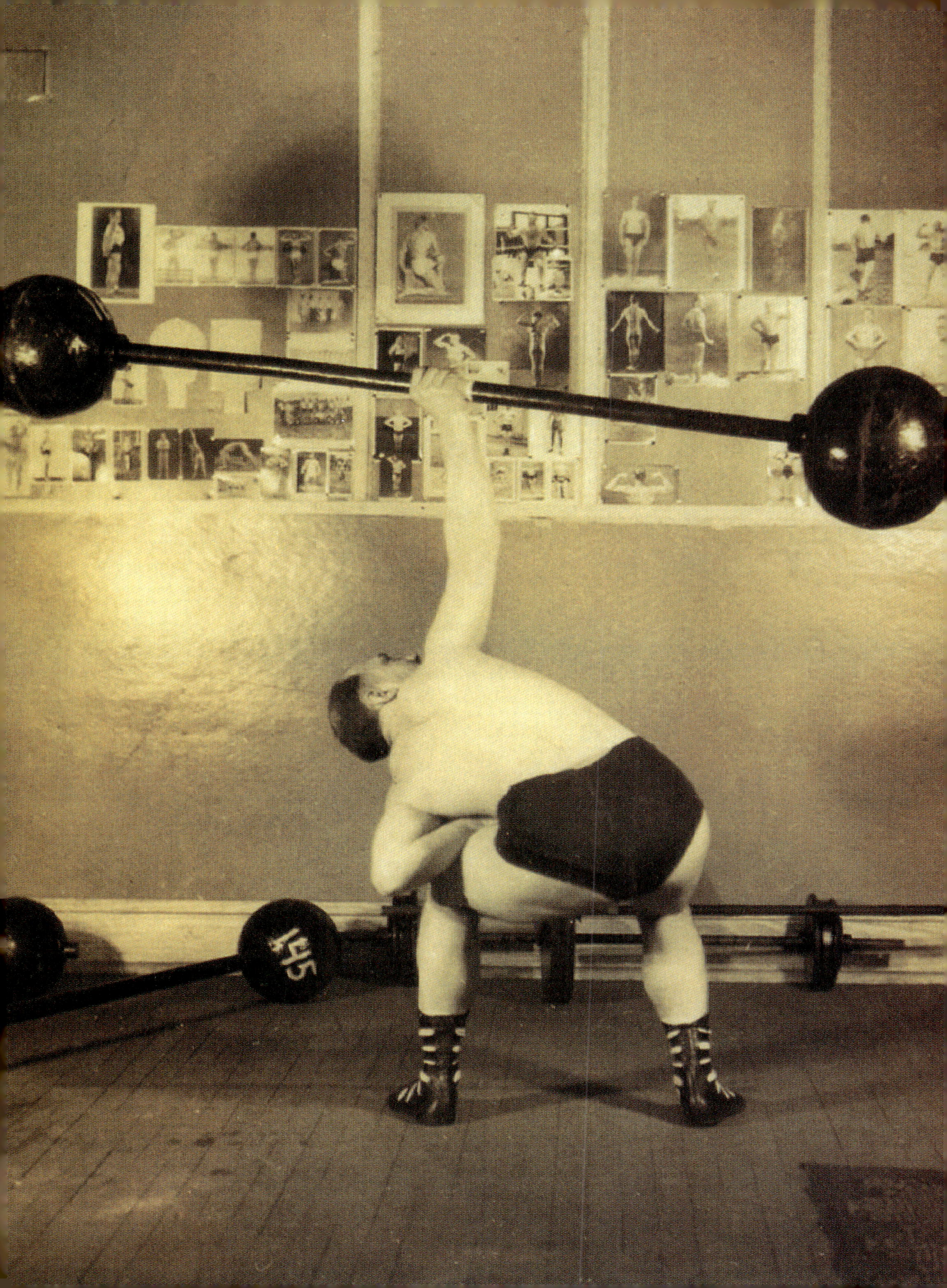

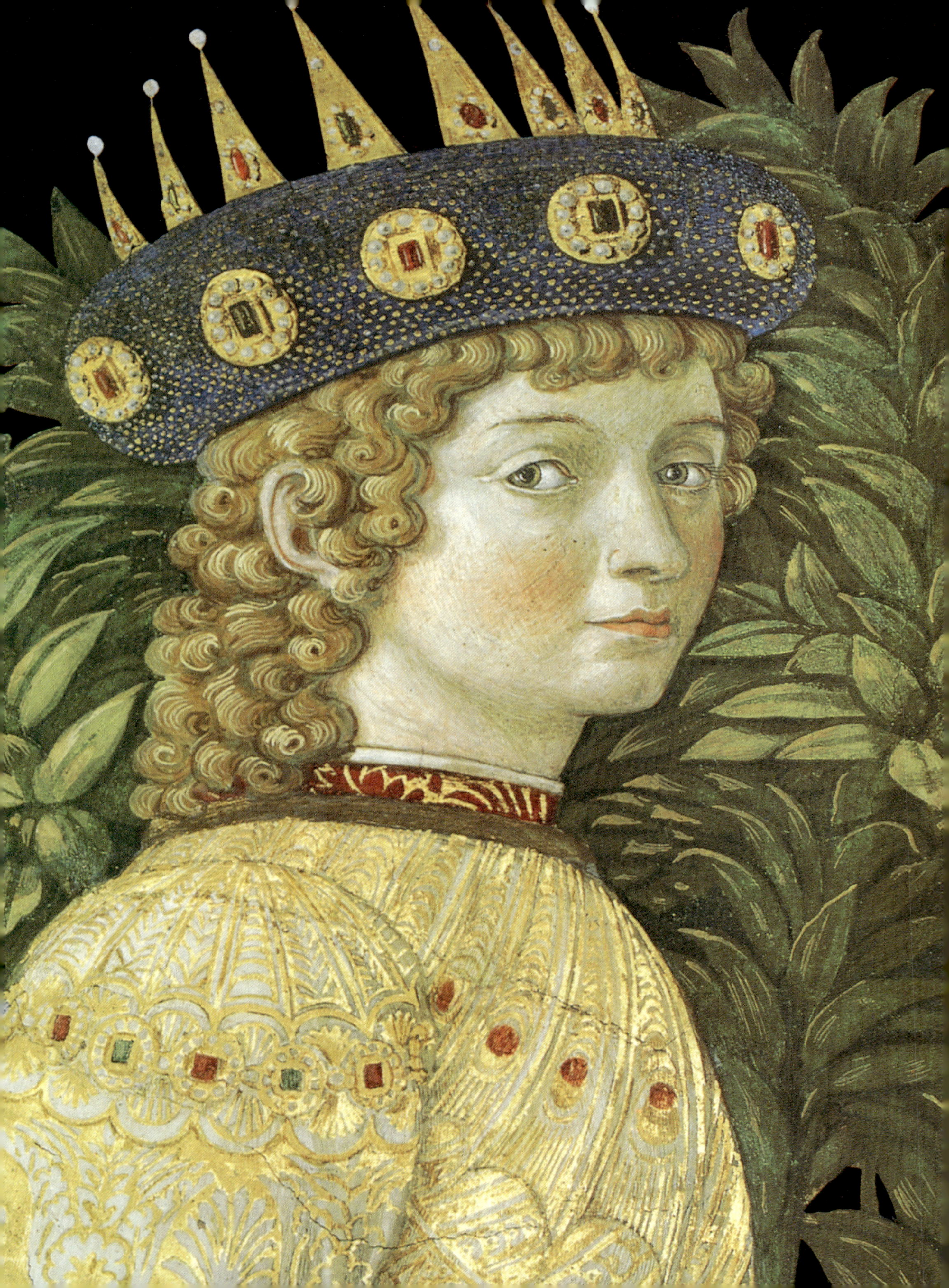

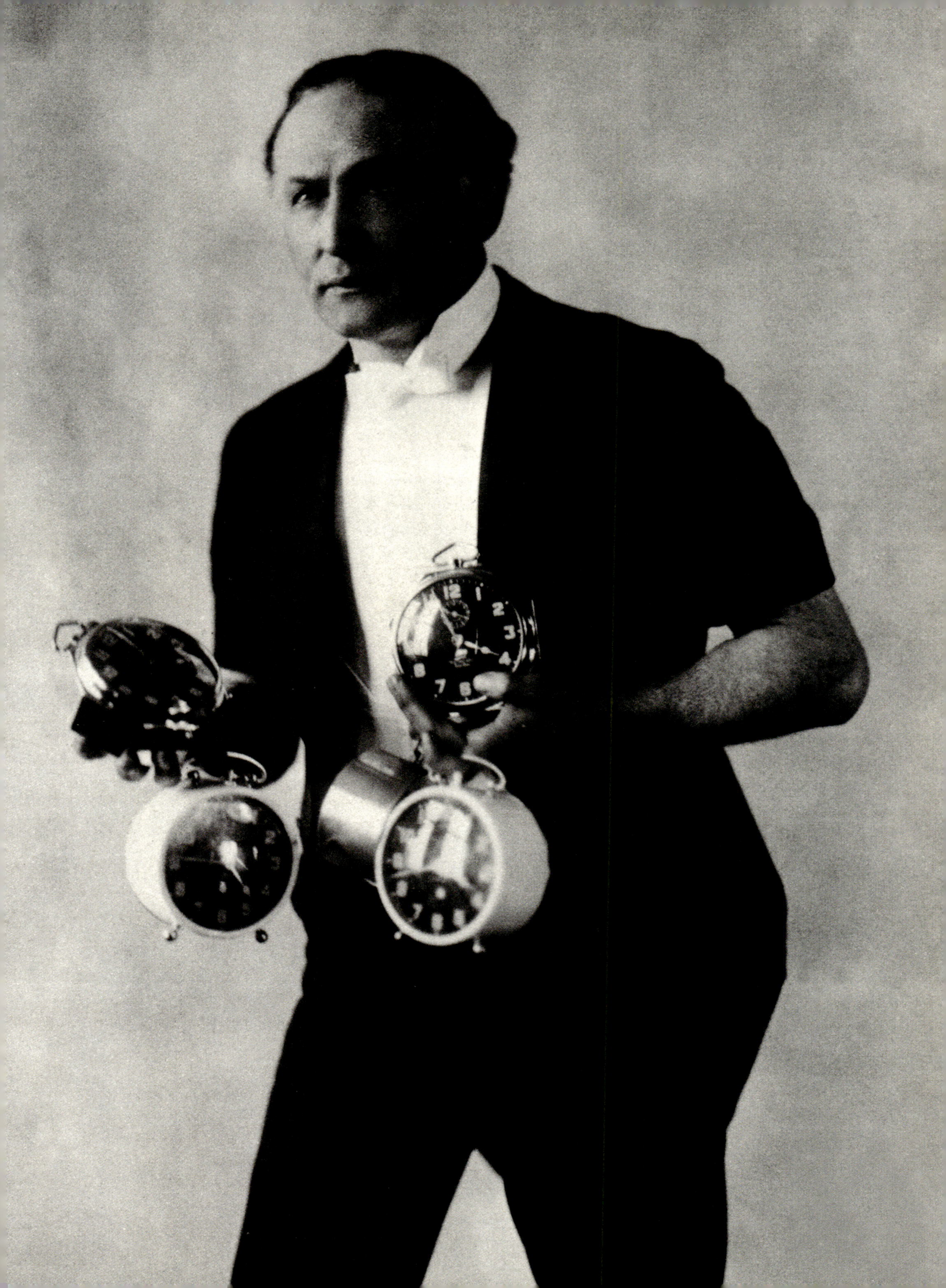

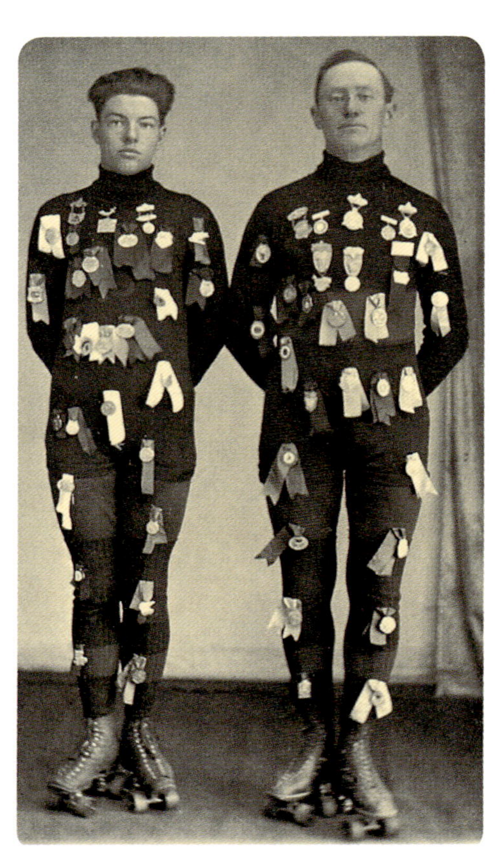

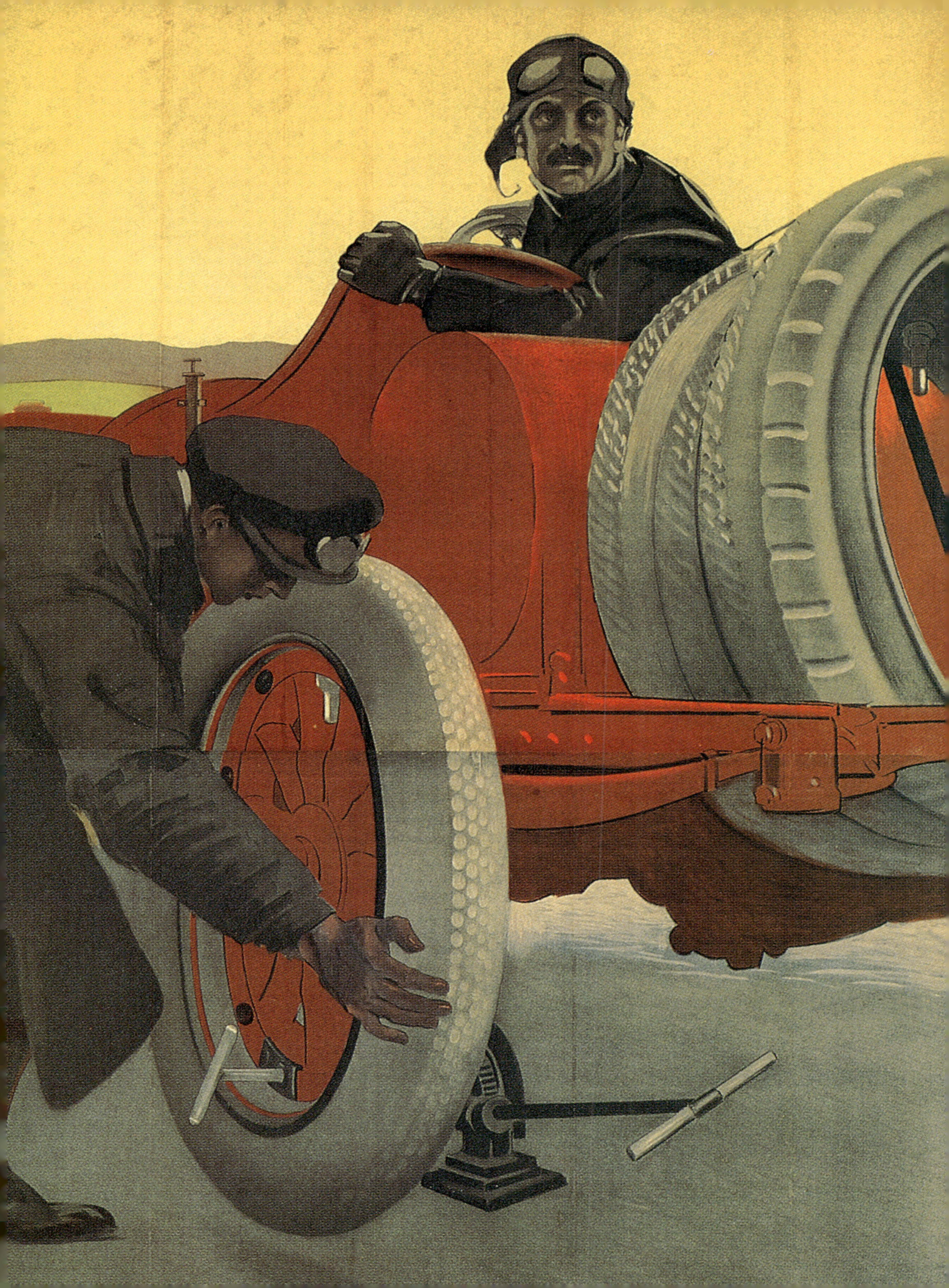

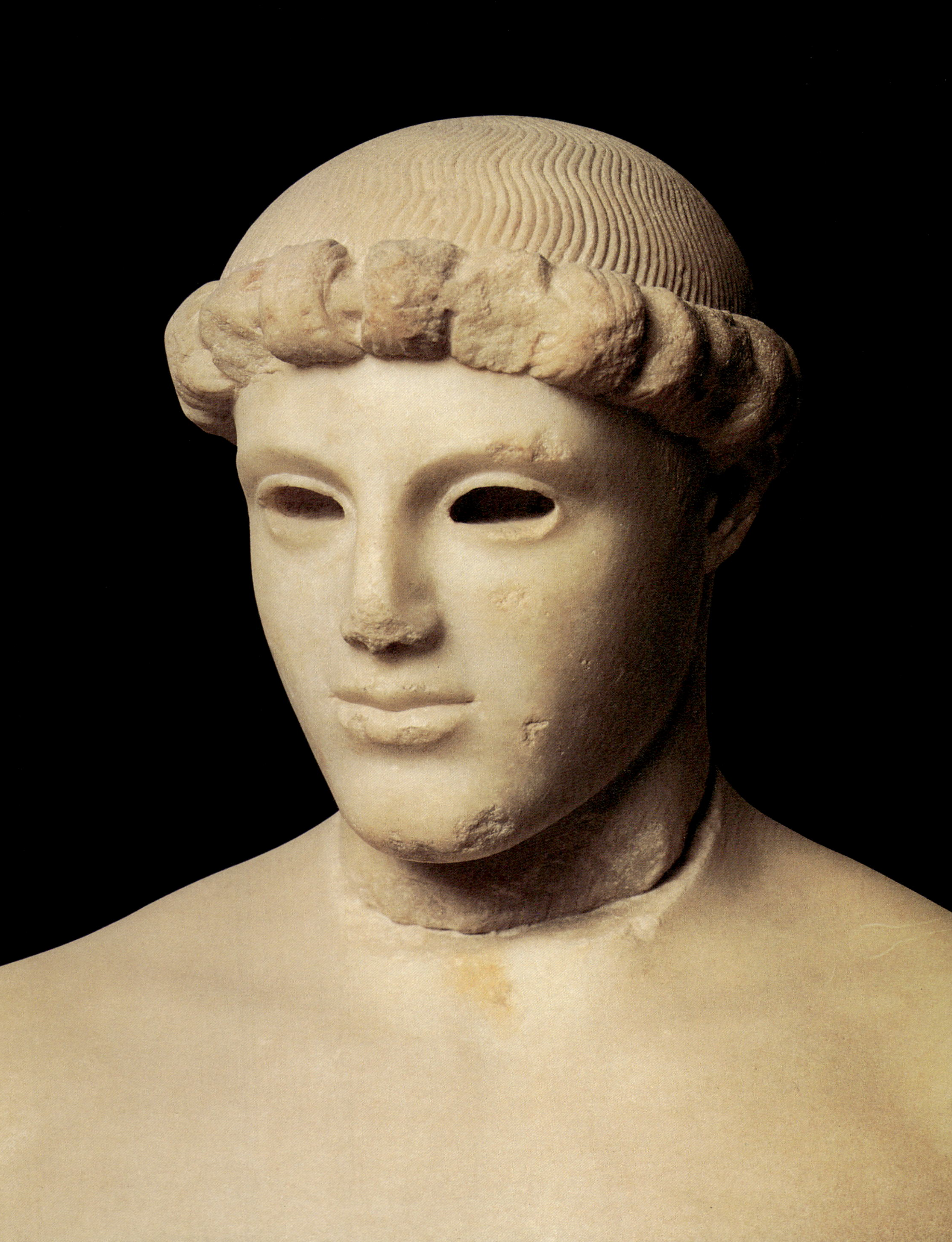

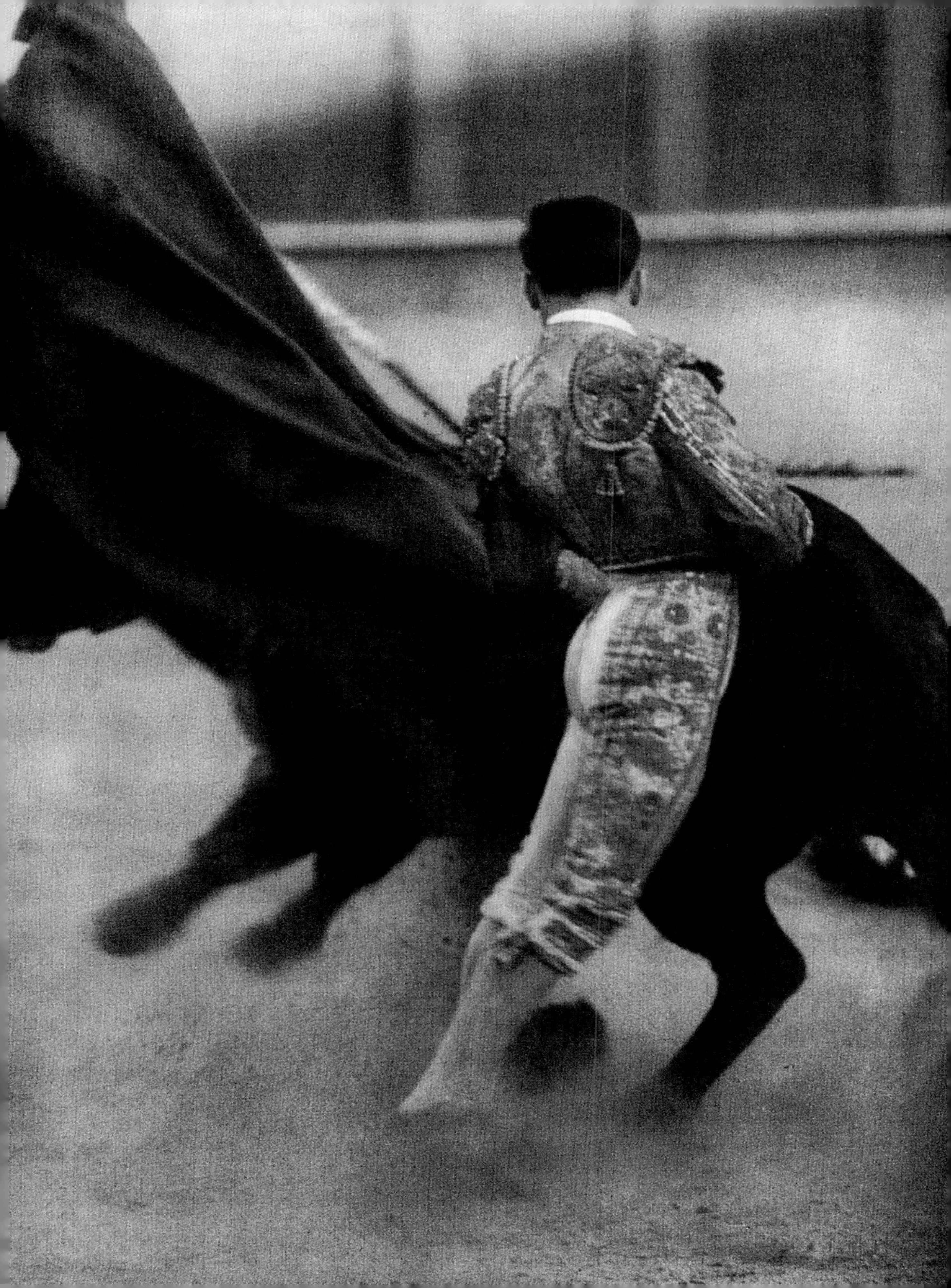

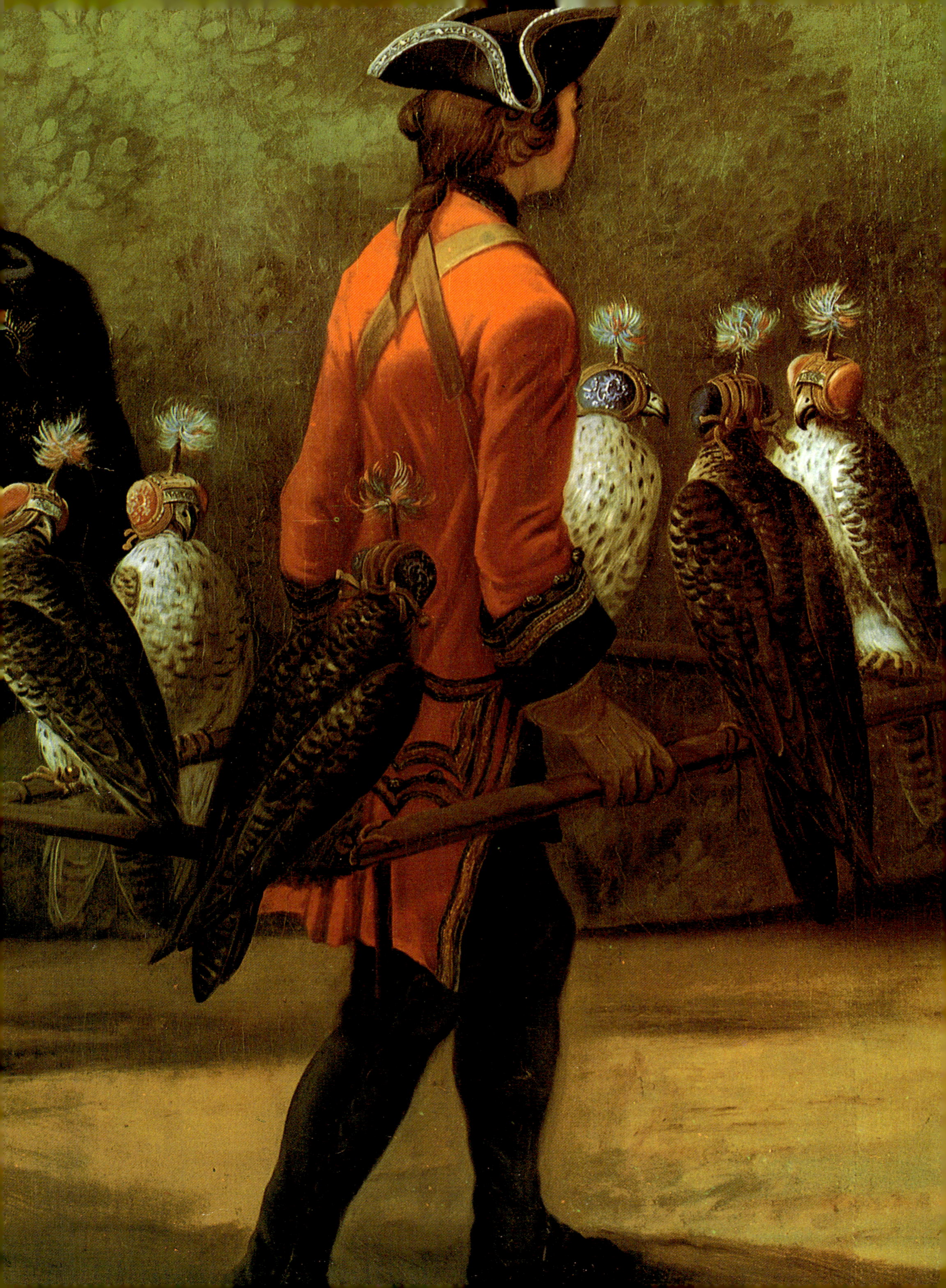

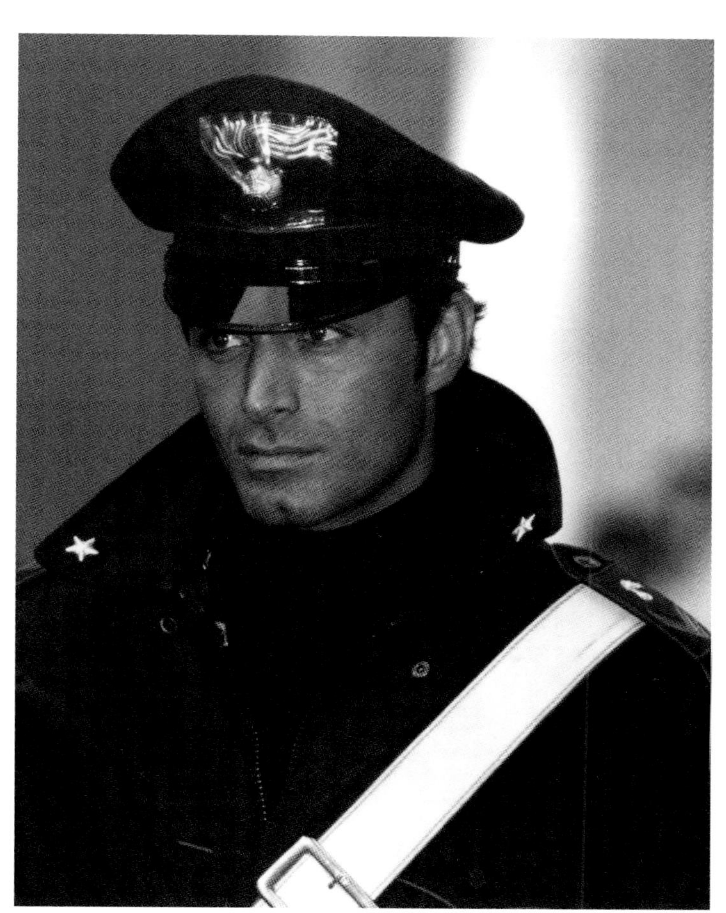

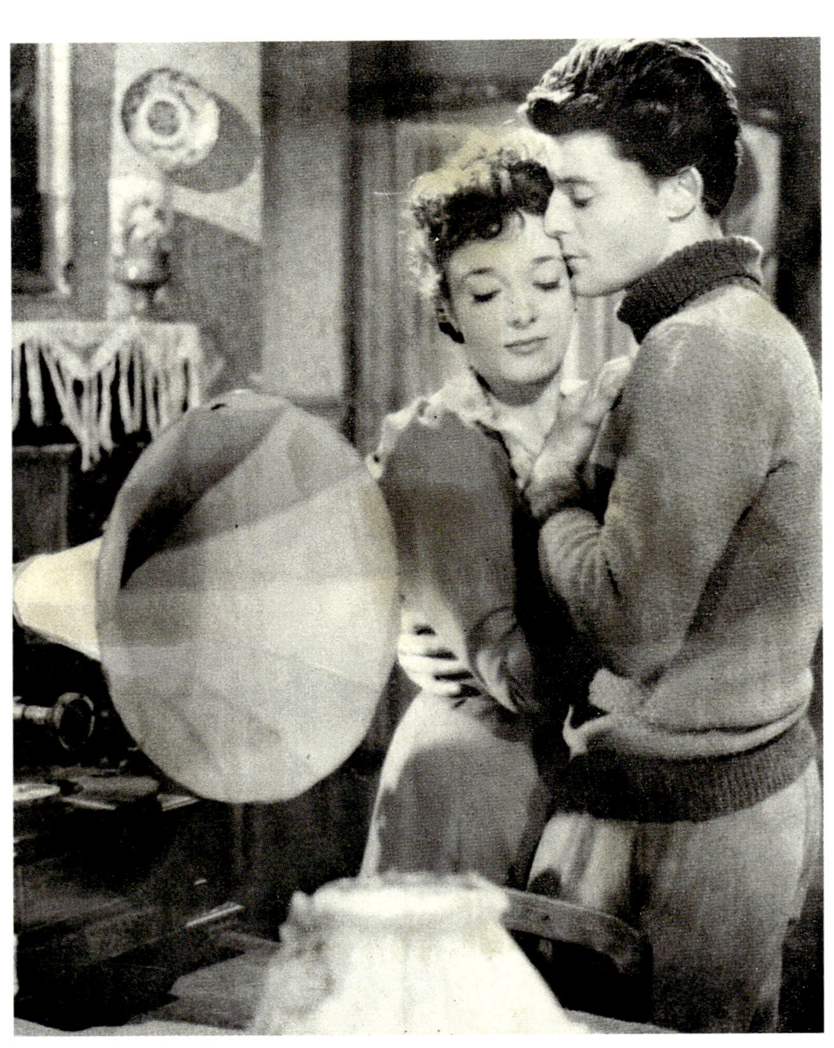

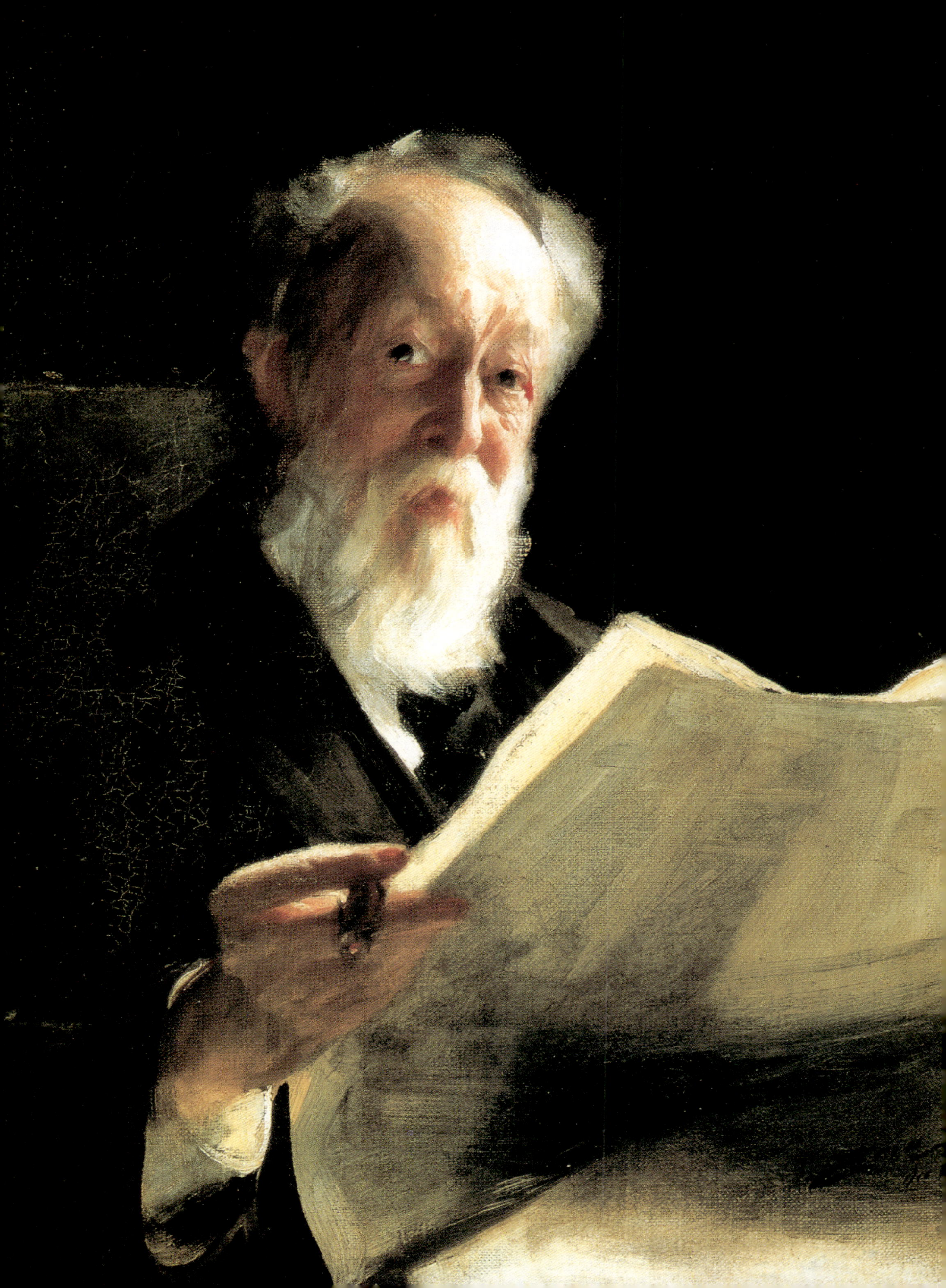

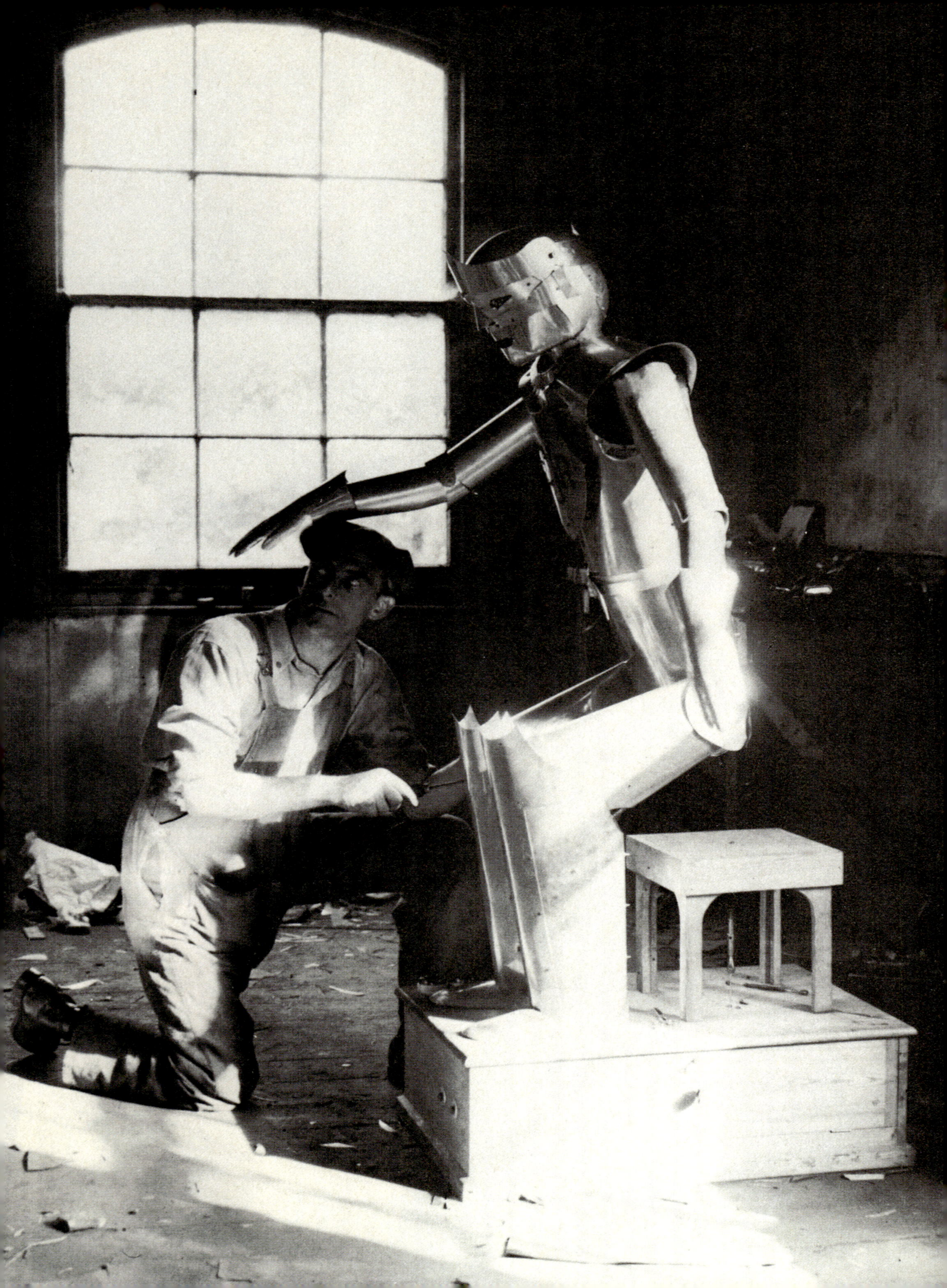

# COLOPHON

PICTURE CREDITS

Cover  Tom Purvis.  London clothier's poster, 1935.

Front flap       Unknown. Photograph of newsboy, c. 1902.

Frontispiece   Walter Carone. Photograph of French actor Jean Gabin, 1949.

3  Casper David Friedrich. "The Wanderer Above The Mists," c. 1818.

4  Plinio Codognato. Fiat poster, 1923.

5  Carl Moll. "Selbstbildnis im atelier," 1906.

6  Unknown. "Hall – Seattle Giants, Pacific Northwest League Baseball," 1911.

7  Marc Vaux.  Amadeo Modigliani, 1918.

8  Raphael. "Baldassare Castiglioni," c. 1500.

9  Unknown. Tin toy, Germany, c. 1950.

10  Unknown. Photograph of newsboy, c. 1902.

11  Pontormo. "Portrait de Cosimo de Medici" (detail), 16th century.

12  Albert Sands Southworth and Josiah Johnson Hawes. Rollin Heber Neal, pastor of the First Baptist Church, Boston, c. 1850.

13  Eleanor Fortescue Brickdale. From *The Book of Old English Songs and Ballads*, 1915.

14  Unknown. Lottery employees ready London for first prize in 1932 contest.

15  N.C. Wyeth. "The Ore Wagon," 1908.

16  Luis Eugenio Meléndez. "Portrait of the Artist Holding A Life Study," 18th century.

17  Unknown. John La Gatta, 1939.

18  Hippolyte Flandrin. "Jeune homme nu assis au bord de la mer," 19th century.

19  Matthew W. Brady or staff.  Lewis Payne, conspirator in the Lincoln assassination plot, 1865.

20  Moriz Nähr.  Gustave Klimt, c. 1912.

21  (quotations)

22  Unknown. Barnum and Bailey circus poster, 1892.

23  Paul Nadar. "Monsieur Holschuch's hat, cane and glove," 1894.

24  Léon Riesener. Daguerreotype of Delacroix, 1842.

25  Unknown. Robot tin toy, c. 1950.

26  Thurston Hopkins. "The Amateur Modelmaker," n.d.

27  José J. Cruz. "Espuelas de Oro," 1947.

28  Unknown. *Meccano* magazine cover, 1930.

29  Dr. Paul Wolff. Olympic Games, 1936.

30  T. Lux Feininger. "The Leap Over The Bauhaus," 1928.

31  Henri de Toulouse-Lautrec. "The Englishman at the Moulin Rouge," 1892.

32  Paul Nadar.  Victor Hugo, c. 1883.

33  Unknown. Snapshot, 1915.

34  Mike Disfarmer.  "I.D. Stark and Bill Stone, cousins" (detail), c. 1940.

35  Anne-Louis Girodet de Roussy-Trioson. "Portrait of Jean-Baptiste Belley," 1797.

36  Unknown.  Alberto Santos Dumont, 1906.

37  Sven Henriksen. "Stjernens Øe og Mineralvande," c. 1932.

38  Unknown. Still from Vittorio de Sica's film *The Bicycle Thief*, 1948.

39  Unknown, n.d.

40  Unknown. Still of Katherine Hepburn and David Manners from George Cukor's film *A Bill of Divorcement*, 1932.

41  (quotations)

42  Rudolph Belarski. *West* magazine cover, 1943.

43  Baron Adolf de Meyer.  Lou Tellegen, c. 1915.

44  Jacques-Louis David. "The Oath of the Horatii," 1784.

45  Harold E. Edgerton. "Wesley Fesler kicks a football," c. 1937.

46  Unknown. Warrior carrying a long sword, Deccan (from a Bijapur workshop), 17th century.

47  Michelangelo. "Giorno" (detail), From the Tomb of Giuliano de Medici, c. 1520-1534.

48  Klokien. Carreras de Motos poster, 1950.

49  Rembrandt. "Self-Portrait," 1629.

# PICTURE CREDITS

50 Unknown. A Franco-British suit of "armor" made for World War I.

51 Gustave Caillebotte. "Raboteurs de parquet," 1876.

52 Unknown, c. 1950.

53 Atelier d'Andrea del Verrocchio. Bust of Piero de Medici, c. 1470.

54 Mrs. Albert Bloom. Privates Raper, Crocket, and Beckham, n.d.

55 Anne-Louis Girodet de Roussy-Trioson. "Portrait of Mustapha," 1819.

56 Unknown. Italian military uniform, n.d.

57 Leon Cremiere. "Les Lutteurs Marseille Frères," c. 1867.

58 Robert Coburn. Charles Boyer, 1937.

59 Utagawa Kuniyoshi. Depiction of Ogata Shuma Hiroyuki, Edo Period (1830-1836).

60 Unknown. Grand Parisy poster, n.d.

61 Brown Brothers. Untitled photograph, n.d.

62 Unknown. Still of Buster Keaton from his film *The Navigator*, 1924.

63 (quotations)

64 Unknown. Snapshot, n.d.

65 Jean-Baptiste-Siméon Chardin. "Portrait of Chardin Wearing an Eyeshade," 1775.

66 Erich Retzlaff. "Blast furnace worker," c. 1931.

67 Christian Krohg. "Karl Nordstrom," 1882.

68 Ludwig Hohlwein. Die Grathnohl-Zigarette poster, 1921.

69 Unknown. Untitled, photograph, n.d.

70 Unknown. Umpire Jack Sheridan, 1905.

71 George Frederick Watts. "Sir Galahad," 1862.

72 Unknown. Untitled, photograph, n.d.

73 Unknown. Nigerian sculpture, c. 12th-14th century.

74 Baron Adolf de Meyer. "Portrait of Ernest," 1938.

75 Emil Nolde. "Self-Portrait," 1917.

76 Unknown. "Samurai wearing formal kimono," c. 1860-1890.

77 Unknown. Albert Camus, 1947.

78 Michelangelo. "David" (detail), c. 1500.

79 Unknown. *All Star Western* comic book cover, 1955.

80 Unknown. Photograph, n.d.

81 Raphael. "Portrait of the Artist with a Friend," c. 1518.

82 J.C. Leyendecker. Arrow Collar advertisement, c. 1913.

83 (quotations)

84 Leonetto Cappiello. Mossant poster, 1938.

85 Frank Rinehart. "Thundercloud, Blackfeet," 1898.

86 Jean-Léon Gérome. "Le Travail de Marbre," 1890.

87 Unknown. Untitled photograph, n.d.

88 Unknown. Egon Schiele, c. 1912.

89 Unknown. "Emmett Farris, Cincinnati, Ohio," 1937.

90 Benozzo Gozzoli. "The Procession of the Magi" (detail), c. 1459.

91 Unknown. Harry Houdini, n.d.

92 Unknown. Untitled photograph from American Photo Gallery, n.d.

93 Marcello Dudovich. Dunlop poster, 1938

94 Unknown. "Statue of a Young: The Kritios Boy," 480-470 B.C.

95 Unknown. Untitled photograph, n.d.

96 Unknown. "The Falconer," 1767.

97 Tamara DiCaprio. "Florence," 2003.

98 Unknown. Gerard Philippe in French film still, n.d.

99 Anders Zorn. "Thomas Wheeler," 1893.

100 Unknown. The robot "Eric" designed by Captain W.H. Richards, 1928.

Back Flap  Plinio Codognato. Fiat poster, 1923.

Back Cover  Erich Retzlaff. "Blast furnace worker," c. 1931.

# RICHARD KEHL

is an artist, teacher, and author. He attended the Kansas City Art Institute where he became so excited about art that "he did not sleep until he was thirty." The Japanese design magazine *Creation* selected him as one of the 100 most interesting graphic designers of the 20th century. He is the author of *The Feminine* (1985), *How to Make a Zero Backwards* (1989) and *Breathing on Your Own* (2002). He collects images, and his hobby is exploring foreign cities.

# THE MASCULINE